JESUS' TWENTY MEGATRUTHS

Herb Miller

Chalice Press
St. Louis, Missouri

Cover: Michael C. Foley

Interior design: Elizabeth Wright

Art Director: Michael A. Domínguez

This book is printed on acid-free, recycled paper.

Visit Chalice Press on the World Wide Web at
www.chalicepress.com

10 9 8 7 6 5 4 3 2 1   98 99 00 01 02 03

Library of Congress Cataloging–in–Publication Data

Miller, Herb.
　　Jesus' twenty megatruths / by Herb Miller.
　　　　p.　cm.
　　Includes bibliographical references.
　　ISBN 0-8272-1712-9
　　　　1. Jesus Christ—Teachings.　2. Kingdom of God—Biblical teaching.　I. Title.
　　BT94.M52　1998　　　　　　　　　　　　　　　　　98–17309
　　230—dc21　　　　　　　　　　　　　　　　　　　　　　CIP

Printed in the United States of America

Dedicated to
the Kellogg, Iowa, congregation,
whose patience and love
helped lay a strong foundation
for ministry

Acknowledgments

Countless pastors at retreats in various parts of the U.S. helped sharpen these insights. Discussion groups in congregations across the country served as test-flight passengers for several chapters. But most of all, thanks be to the Nazareth Carpenter, who first said it all.

Contents

Introduction

Jesus taught only one thing about how to live a quality life: the kingdom of God. But Jesus illustrated that megatruth in twenty different ways. This explains most of the controversies about his teachings. Jesus' great mind could see all twenty slices of truth simultaneously. You and I can rarely manage more than two or three. Because of (a) childhood training, (b) personal experiences, (c) the social conditions of our generation, and (d) the spiritual perception lenses common in our particular culture, each of us tends to focus in on those few teachings. Though we have read the New Testament, we hardly know that the other sixteen or eighteen teachings of Jesus exist. If we do, we assume that he barely mentioned them or that they are unimportant. We therefore spend our years reading and rereading our "mentally abridged edition" of what Jesus taught about how to live a quality life. This myopic perception can produce distorted thinking, distorted behavior, and distorted denominations. It allows us to read the words and obtain only a piece of the Word—while the remainder stands in a stack of leather-bound pages on our mantel, waiting to be appropriated.

Personal Distortions: Get a picture of your own "theological selectivity" by completing either individually or as part of a group the "Personal Opinion Survey Regarding Jesus' Twenty Megatruths" in the Appendix. After completing that, compare it with the "Annotated List of Jesus' Twenty Megatruths," also found in the Appendix. Yes, we all start from exactly the same source. But each of us unknowingly selects a different emphasis.

Denominational Distortions: Ask five ministers and five adult Sunday school classes in five denominations to complete and discuss the "Personal Opinion Survey Regarding Jesus' Twenty Megatruths" found in the Appendix. This will illustrate why all denominations say they base their beliefs

1

on the Bible, yet come up with entirely different views and wonder why other Christians cannot see things as clearly as they do.

Generational Distortions: Reading sermons or Christian education material from earlier decades feels like walking through a museum of Christian thought. They, too, worked at presenting the Nazareth Carpenter's ideas, but how different they sound! Why? Theological selectivity! The experiences through which each generation passes on its way to maturity cause it to "select out" those teachings that seem to need greater emphasis. This is why older and younger church members and ministers can disagree so radically, yet sincerely.

Our generation is not the first to select a new emphasis from among Jesus' teachings. G. K. Chesterton said, "Each generation is converted by the saint who contradicts it most."[+] Medieval Catholic St. Francis of Assisi became popular in England because its people felt the previous generation had neglected the merits he advocated. Several hundred years later, Christians in the 1930s began responding to the rational theology of St. Thomas because they felt the previous generation had neglected reason.

This is one of the reasons why Bible study is so important and why spiritual renewal in both individuals and churches is always accompanied by a renewal of Bible study and Bible study groups. Through that experience we learn what Jesus really taught about how to build a quality life—rather than what we have assumed he taught.

This study/discussion book is designed to correct many of the theological distortions toward which all Christians unconsciously tend. It will not tell us everything Jesus *meant* by what he taught. No book can do that. But it can bring us a balanced view of the twenty ways Jesus says the kingdom of God helps people live quality lives in a variety of changing circumstances.

+*St. Thomas Aquinas* by G. K. Chesterton (New York: Doubleday, 1933), p. 24.

1

Some Realities Are Invisible

A navy veteran once described the aura of greatness that surrounded a famous admiral. Hero of countless battles with the Germans in the Mediterranean and numerous convoy landings in the South Pacific, the great leader had one idiosyncrasy. Each morning after breakfast he went to his stateroom, opened the safe, and read from a small piece of paper. After he retired from active service, someone looked in the safe and found the little note he had read every day. It said, "Starboard is right. Port is left."

The most basic truth Jesus taught is also the easiest to forget. It, too, comes in a three-word package: *God is here*. All his other ideas stem from this assumption, like the shiny spokes of a bicycle wheel grow out of its axle. In trying to communicate this central megatruth, Jesus used another three-word phrase more than 110 times in the New Testament records: *kingdom of God*. Jesus said God is here and you experience him by entering what he called the "kingdom of God." These six words are so much the center of Jesus' teachings that perhaps we should write them down, store the paper in a safe place, and read it every morning: *God is here. Enter the kingdom.*

Biblical scholars at every point on the theological compass agree on Jesus' central message. Across the centuries, however, definitions and explanations of that central term have achieved far less consensus among scholars. Hundreds of books have attempted to explain it, through the use of various metaphors and analogies. Each of these, at different moments in history, has made a contribution to Christian thinking about Jesus' term, kingdom of God.

Many scholars, however, recognize the indefinable nature of Jesus' term. The kingdom of God describes a phenomenon that lies mostly outside the range of human explanation. Therefore, using a metaphor (a figure of speech that denotes likeness between one kind of object or idea and another completely different object or idea) is the only way we can discuss the kingdom of God.

One kingdom metaphor that makes sense to many contemporary laypersons is "new level of consciousness." Every human being experiences shifts in level of consciousness. Consider these examples:

- Do you remember the first time you fell in love? The day that happened, you became an entirely different person. Everything changed. Your thinking and behavior suddenly came under the control of a whole new perspective. You looked at the world through a new mental window. You had entered a new "level of consciousness."

- Anger is another level of consciousness that changes your perspective. During the moments when you are caught in the grip of anger, your thinking and behavior temporarily shift to different gears. You become a different person than you were before.

- Fear is another level of consciousness. What was the most frightening situation you ever experienced? During that time, was your thinking about what is important and what is unimportant radically altered? You were still the same person—yet you were not the same person. All your motives, aspirations, and priorities were momentarily reshuffled.

- Depression or "the blues" is yet another level of consciousness. When you are in the grip of that deadening mood, you look at the world through negative-colored glasses. Your "apperceptive set" has been temporarily restructured.

What was Jesus asking Peter to do that day at the seashore when he said, "Follow me"? What was he asking Matthew to do that day at the tax office in Capernaum when he said, "Follow me"? He was inviting both of them to enter a new level of consciousness that would change their perspectives, priorities, and behaviors.

That happens to every person who experiences Christian conversion. With some people, this comes instantly. With others, the process is slower. But every type of conversion has a beginning point. At a particular moment in time, the person enters a new level of consciousness in which God and his truths become a part of life orientation. Jesus called this "entering the kingdom of God."

Warning: Do not confuse the metaphor "new level of consciousness" with New Age movement thinking or other contemporary distortions of biblical Christian thought. Like all metaphors, "level of consciousness" is not precisely synonymous with Jesus' term "kingdom of God." It is, however, one meaningful way to describe the psychological state of persons who enter the kingdom of God that Jesus described. Like all metaphors, "new level of consciousness" is a limited rather than a comprehensive description. The kingdom of God is far more than a personal state of mind; it is the entire realm of God's sovereignty—past, present, and future—both in the world that we can see with our eyes and in the world beyond that we cannot see. To say that the kingdom of God is *only* a psychological level of consciousness would imply that it has no objective reality outside our own thought patterns. According to the New Testament, the kingdom of God is an objective reality, not a subjective experience in our imagination that does not exist until we decide it exists.

Do we become Christians by making a rational decision, or is this an emotional decision? Yes and no. Both and neither. Becoming a disciple of Jesus Christ is *beyond* rationality and emotionality. It means new birth into a new level of consciousness in which we see the world from a new perspective. When Jesus announced the "good news of the kingdom," he was saying, "God is here, and when you enter his kingdom you enter a new level of consciousness. This makes possible completely new kinds of thinking and behavior."

Some argue that Jesus' central idea was "God is love." That is almost true, but not quite. Of what value would God be if he is loving, yet distant? Jesus said God is both here and love, but God's presence is Jesus' most basic teaching. A God of love who is distant— somewhere in the sky or tied up with religious rituals at the

MEGATRUTH ONE

You experience new ways of thinking and behavior when you enter God's kingdom.

temple—would hold little significance. But a God who is *here,* that is big news—good news, new news—the best of all good news possibilities.

How can this be? How can God be everywhere at once? Every day the air around us is surrounded with radio waves—several different ones. If you switch on a radio receiver, you enter the kingdom of radio waves. And do not the words you hear often begin to modify your thinking and behavior? Jesus says there is much more in the air around us than radio waves.

Megatruth Number One: *You experience new ways of thinking and behavior when you enter God's kingdom.* Here are a few examples from the statements of Jesus recorded in the New Testament: In Luke 17:20–21, he says that the kingdom of God is present now "among you." In Luke 11:20, he tells people that the kingdom of God has already come upon them.

In Luke 12:32, he says, "Do not be afraid, little flock, for it is your Father's good pleasure to give you the kingdom." In John 3:3, he says, "Very truly, I tell you, no one can see the kingdom of God without being born from above." In John 3:4–8, he says we don't know where the wind comes from or where it goes, and so it is with those born of the Spirit. In Matthew 19:14, he makes it clear that great religious knowledge is not a requirement for those who wish to enter the kingdom of God; it is available to everyone and we enter it with the naiveté of a child. In Matthew 13:1–9, his parable of the soils seems to indicate that this new state of consciousness comes to different people in different degrees.

This megatruth is the basic theological foundation under all Christian denominations. Last Sunday morning, the doors of approximately 375,000 special buildings opened across North America and more than 90 million people entered to spend an hour or so. The pope of the Roman Catholic Church occasionally issues statements listened to with respect by most of the sixty million Catholics in the United States. Last week, more than 13,500 infants had a few drops of water scattered across their heads by a special person in a special robe. Last week, more than 8,000 young people and adults were dipped beneath the surface of a special vat of water in a place of worship. The thinking and actions of all these persons were greatly influenced by this, Jesus' most basic teaching.

Megatruth Number One is a bit like the bread which always accompanies an American meal. It is always present, but nobody remarks much about it. When people describe a particular denomination, they usually do so in terms of its emphasis on one or more of Jesus' *other* nineteen megatruths—just as they would describe a meal by the main course or the dessert. But Megatruth Number One is always present. Without it, Christianity ceases to be Christianity and drifts off into animism (belief that gods inhabit trees and rocks), rationalism (belief that our minds are gods), or that God is only a set of philosophical principles.

When Abraham set out from his home in Haran more than three thousand years ago, he was betting his life on this principle. He was responding to a voice telling him to go to a place he had never seen before and build a great nation, even though he was already an old man. Abraham heard what others did not hear. He felt what others could not feel. He had entered a new level of consciousness. He knew that God is here. The saints of the Church through all the ages—from Saint Augustine to Saint Francis to Joan of Arc—have clung stolidly to this megatruth, often in the face of extreme persecution.

There is either more to this world than meets the eye, or what you see is what you get. God is either here, or he isn't. Jesus says he is. Many say he isn't. What do you say?

Discovery Questions for Group Discussion

1. Read Matthew 22:15–22 (also found in Mark 12:13–17 and Luke 20:20–26). Jesus says we should recognize that God is here, just as we recognize that our civil government is here. Thinking back over the past week, list some things that you did, said, or thought that seem to be based on the assumption that God is here. List some things you saw or heard about in the lives of other people that seem to be based on this assumption.

2. Read Luke 17:20–21. If the kingdom of God is already here, how do you explain the existence of evil in the world?

3. Read Luke 11:20. Jesus says he deals with evil through the presence of God. Can you give examples of people today dealing with evil in the same way?

4. Read Luke 12:32. Jesus says entering the kingdom is a gift, not something we earn. This sounds similar to Martin Luther's historic statement that "salvation is by

faith alone." If that is the case, what is the point of trying to live a morally upright life?

5. Read John 3:1–8. If we enter the kingdom only by the invisible power of the Spirit, what is the use of going to church and participating in other Christian activities?

6. Read John 6:60–65. If no one can come into the kingdom except by the gift of God, what is the point of all the efforts Christians put forth to do evangelism?

7. Read Mark 12:28–30 and Mark 12:32–34 (also found in Matthew 22:35–38, 40 and Luke 10:25–28). Jesus seems to say that the primary means by which we enter the kingdom is by loving God. What do you think he means by the term "love God"?

8. Read Matthew 19:14. If all we need in order to enter the kingdom is the naiveté of a child, why bother to study the Bible?

9. Read Luke 8:16–18 and Luke 11:33–36 (also found in Mark 4:21–23). What do you think Jesus means by these two parables about light?

10. Read Matthew 4:10 (also found in Luke 4:8). In what ways is Jesus' statement from the story of his temptation in the wilderness similar to the two previous parables about light?

11. Read Matthew 13:31–32 (also found in Mark 4:30–32 and Luke 13:18–19) and Matthew 13:33 (also found in Luke 13:20–21). If the kingdom is a new level of consciousness, how can it grow like a seed or leaven in the way described in these texts?

12. Read Matthew 13:1–9 (also found in Mark 4:3–9, 20 and Luke 8:4–11, 15). The parable of soils seems to indicate that people enter the new level of consciousness called the kingdom of God in different degrees. Do you agree or disagree with that idea? Illustrate.

13. Do you think some Christians carry this megatruth to dangerous extremes? Illustrate.
14. Do you think some Christians tend to disregard this megatruth completely? Illustrate.
15. Do you think people in your denomination believe and practice this megatruth more, less, or about the same as forty years ago? Illustrate.

Additional Examples

In the first words we hear Jesus utter in the gospel records, he says he must be in his Father's house. (Luke 2:49)

Jesus says that his baptism by John is a fitting way to recognize God's righteousness. (Matthew 3:15)

Jesus prays for the kingdom to come and God's will to be done on earth as it is in heaven. (Matthew 6:9–10 and Luke 11:2)

Jesus says he speaks in parables and that many cannot see the kingdom. (Matthew 13:10–17; Mark 4:10–12, 24–25; and Luke 8:10)

Jesus says the kingdom is like a treasure hidden in a field. (Matthew 13:44) Jesus says the kingdom is like a merchant who finds a pearl of great value. (Matthew 13:45–46)

Jesus says a scribe of the kingdom uses both old traditions and new ideas. (Matthew 13:51–52)

In his triple parables of the lost coin, the lost sheep, and the lost son, Jesus says God is here and seeks even those persons who don't have the desire or ability to seek him. (Luke 15:1–32)

The thief on the cross beside Jesus recognizes and enters the kingdom during the last moment of his life. (Luke 23:39–43)

2

You Gotta Have Heart

The boy grew up in a large, downtown church. Renowned across the country as one of the best in the denomination, the church had a multiple staff and strong preaching from one of the pulpit greats. Excellent programing and well-organized youth events strengthened its reputation. The boy was quite active in the congregation. He attended pastor's class, was baptized at age thirteen, served as president of the youth group, and was active in regional youth structures. Married in the church, he attended regularly while starting a family and became a church officer. He and his wife gave a healthy percentage of their income to philanthropic causes.

Then, in a series of totally unexpected events, his life started unraveling at all four corners. The stresses he hadn't had before arrived in a bundle. His business failed. He took bankruptcy in an agony of embarrassment. The marriage deteriorated and began breaking apart. His parents divorced after thirty years, saying they had never loved each other. His six-year-old son received a leukemia diagnosis two days before Christmas.

Desperate for something to hold his life together, he attended a weekend men's retreat to which he had been invited by a friend in another denomination. The speaker unfolded some old truths in new ways. They entered his mind like mercury vapor lamps in a coal mine. When he left the retreat on Sunday afternoon, he said he would never be the same again. He wasn't. Life changed for the better. He had found a totally new perspective. Ten years later, he still had it. "I don't understand why nobody told me these things before," he said. "My own church should have helped me find this kind of faith."

An old story tells of a little boy who grew up far out in the country earlier in this century. On one of the family's infrequent trips to town for supplies, he saw a poster announcing that a circus was coming to town. Never having seen a circus, he saved his money and counted the days. He was so excited on the last night that he could hardly sleep. By the crack of dawn he was on his pony riding toward town. Standing along the street in the crowd, he watched the circus parade. Amazed at the tigers, lions, and bears, his eyes grew even wider as he saw the elephants, acrobats, jugglers, clowns, and the circus band.

MEGATRUTH TWO

You enter God's kingdom only by a changed attitude of the heart, not by following a list of religious rules.

When the end of the passing drama came into sight, he stepped out of the crowd, handed the money he had saved to the last marcher, got on his pony, and rode home. It wasn't until a couple of years later that he realized he had missed the main event in the big top. He had gone to see the circus but had only watched the parade.

Jesus warned that this is one of the great dangers of organized religion. We can get into God's house without getting to God. We can do a lot of good things without doing the main thing. Megatruth Number Two: *You enter God's kingdom only by a changed attitude of the heart, not by following a list of religious rules.*

Jesus recognized the Jewish Law and the "tradition of the elders"—the rabbinical exposition of the Law—as important means to an end. They can help us achieve God-consciousness. But Jesus says we must not stop there. This is the parade—not the main event. Here are a few examples from his teachings: "You hypocrites! Isaiah prophesied rightly about you when he said: 'This people honors me with their lips, but their hearts are far from me; in vain do they worship me, teaching human precepts as doctrines'" (Matthew 15:7–9). In Luke 18:9–14, he contrasts the phony righteousness of the Pharisees who followed all the religious rules with the obvious virtue of a tax collector who had followed no rules but changed his heart. In Luke 16:14–16, he says that the Jewish Law was preached until John the baptizer came, but now the kingdom of God is proclaimed. In Matthew 12:1–14, he permits his disciples to break the Old Testament rules against grain gathering and healing on the Sabbath, then defends himself against his critics by saying that rules are not as important as attitudes and motivations. In Matthew 15:1–20, he says that eating taboo foods does not make people as ritually unclean in God's sight as some of the words they spit out of their mouths, because the words reflect the state of their hearts. In Matthew 16:11–12, he speaks of the bad yeast of the Pharisees and Sadducees, who stress good rituals more than good hearts and lives. In Matthew 10:1–16, he uses a story of vineyard laborers hired at different times during the day to show that the kingdom is freely given by God to those who choose to enter it; we don't earn it by following religious rules for prescribed periods of time. In Matthew 23:23–28, he speaks of the hypocrisy of religious rules without the practice of mercy, honesty, and justice in our relationships with other people.

This teaching of Jesus is probably better illustrated by its perversion in various denominations than by shining examples of groups that follow it thoroughly. A good many denominations were born as a reaction to such errors of omission in their mother churches. The most obvious historical example is the Lutheran Church of sixteenth-century Germany. Under the leadership of young Martin Luther, it broke ranks with the Roman Catholic Church by rebelling against the sale of indulgences. In one of the most despicable and extreme of legalisms, the church hierarchy was selling certificates, signed by the pope himself, purporting to bestow the pardon of all sins. These "indulgences" were pronounced valid not only for the holders of the certificates, but for friends living or dead in whose behalf they were purchased. Confession, repentance, penance, or absolution by a priest was conveniently unnecessary. Tetzal, the church official against whom Luther rebelled, said, "As soon as your coin clinks in the chest, the souls of your friends will rise out of purgatory to heaven." Little wonder that Luther's theological keystone became "by faith alone," a phrase which he took from an early chapter in Paul's letter to the Romans (which Paul had borrowed from Jesus' teaching to and against the Pharisees on this same subject).

Many Baptist groups have followed the Lutheran suit on this matter, insisting that a "born again" experience is the basic key to a relationship with God. In recent years, they seem to have made a great deal of progress in communicating that idea to the public. A 1996 Gallup Poll reports that 35 percent of the U.S. population describe themselves as having had a "born again" experience. This contrasts sharply with the 20 percent who said that in 1963.

Studies among young adults in our society illustrate another dimension of this same concept. A large segment of the new generation that came of age in the 1960s and 1970s can be described as "believers but not belongers." They do not trust the institutional systems of the past—political, social, economic, military, or spiritual—in the same way their parents did. Many see themselves as being religious but have not affiliated in an official way with any church. Religious labels and tradition packages are not too important to them;

it's the heart that counts. They depend much more on their own inner feelings about God and what is right than on what the pope, a preacher, or local church tradition say.

In still a different way, the Charismatic renewal movement which began to sweep through all the denominations in the early 1960s teaches the same thing: the relationship of the heart to God, not the following of religious ritual or tradition, is the main matter. Some heart trouble requires surgery. Some heart trouble requires medication. Some heart trouble requires a pacemaker. Some heart trouble requires a transplant. The kind Jesus talked about can be treated at low risk on an outpatient basis. The procedure has only one requirement: a willing candidate.

Discovery Questions for Group Discussion

1. Read Matthew 23:23–38 (also found in Luke 11:37–44). Jesus does not so much condemn the Jewish traditions, like tithing, as he criticizes them for doing only these things while neglecting other important things, like justice, mercy, and faith. Try to make a list of the important things you believe Christians are most inclined to neglect today.

2. Read Matthew 16:5–12 (also found in Mark 8:13–21). In your opinion, can any teachings of religious leaders today be compared to those of the Pharisees and Sadducees that Jesus warned the disciples about? Illustrate.

3. Read Mark 7:1–23 (also found in Matthew 15:1–11, 15–20). Jesus makes it clear that ritual and tradition are not as important as the heart. Why, then, do you think Jesus felt it important that he be baptized by John in the Jordan River? Why do you think that it was his custom to attend the synagogue services?

4. Read Luke 6:43–45 (also found in Matthew 12:33–35). Jesus indicates that thinking and behavior always grow out of the condition of the heart. If you were put in charge of changing a person's heart for the better, what methods would you recommend for that process?

5. Read Matthew 12:1–8 (also found in Mark 2:23–28 and Luke 6:1–5). This text, and others like it, has been used to justify not attending worship on Sunday. Do you agree or disagree with that interpretation? Why?

6. Read John 4:16–30. Jesus tells the Samaritan woman at the well that those who enter the kingdom do so through spirit and truth, not through the religious rituals of the Jews in Jerusalem or the Samaritans who broke away from the Jews to establish another set of rituals and traditions and worship on a different mountain. Jesus illustrated this truth in his very act of talking publicly with a *woman*—something no pious Jew would do—and especially with a woman of the despised Samaritan religious tradition. Do you think there are any ways in which this text speaks to the matter of our hundreds of different denominations in America today? Illustrate.

7. Do you think some Christians carry this megatruth to dangerous extremes? Illustrate.

8. Do you think some Christians tend to disregard this megatruth completely? Illustrate.

9. During the past few years, do you believe American denominations have been practicing this megatruth more, less, or about the same as in previous decades of this century? Give reasons for your opinion.

10. Some say the way Christians use words and phrases can become as much a ritual or tradition as anything the so-called "high church" denominations do in worship ceremonies at the front of their churches. Do you agree or disagree? Illustrate.

Additional Examples

Jesus says the religious leaders' hearts caused them to fail to see the kingdom of God about which John the Baptist spoke. (Matthew 17:10–13; 11:12–15; and Mark 9:11–13)

Jesus says that he has not come to abolish the Law but to fulfill it—but he warns that righteousness must be of the heart, not just the rules. (Matthew 5:17–24; and Luke 16:14–17)

Jesus says the heart is important in what we do, not the words by which we swear an oath. (Matthew 5:33–37; and 23:16–22)

Jesus says adultery is a matter of the heart. (Matthew 5:27–28, 31–32; 19:3–12; Mark 10:2–12; and Luke 16:18)

Jesus says having the mercy to heal the man with the withered hand is more important than keeping the Sabbath rules. (Matthew 12:9–14; Mark 3:1–6; and Luke 6:6–11)

Jesus heals a woman on the Sabbath and says that helping people is more important than following religious rules. (Luke 13:10–17; 14:1–6)

After healing the paralyzed man on the Sabbath, Jesus says religious traditions are not as important as caring about people. (John 5:1–18)

Referring to his healing of a man on the Sabbath, Jesus urges people to judge actions by whether they help people and not by whether they are consistent with religious traditions. (John 7:21–24)

Jesus says he has sheep (the Gentiles) in other pens, inferring that the disciples should not get puffed up with pride over their role as his followers, any more than the

Jews should feel they are God's chosen people because they have followed his rules and rituals. (John 10:16)

Jesus says the kingdom of God comes to others, not just those of the Hebrew tradition. (Matthew 15:21–27; and Mark 7:24–28)

A person unknown to Jesus and his disciples is found driving out demons in his name, but Jesus says he should be permitted to continue. (Mark 9:38–41)

Jesus says people from all countries and races will enter God's kingdom; many will come from east and west and sit down at the table with Abraham and Isaac. (Matthew 8:11–12; and Luke 13:29)

3

The Christ Connection

The president of a trucking company carries two different business cards—one for general purposes and the other for special situations. The special card looks like any standard business card on the front. On the back it says: "If we meet and you forget me, you have lost nothing. But if you meet Jesus Christ and forget him, you have lost everything."

Another layman says, "The biblical concept of being 'in Christ' is far superior to our contemporary idea of trying to be 'Christlike' in our behavior. When we are 'in Christ,' it is he who decides, speaks, and acts. Rather than us trying to become him in the world, he becomes us in the world."

Both these laymen are echoing an idea which during the past ten years has grown stronger in seminaries of every denomination. Many young pastors are placing greater emphasis on the "person of Christ" and finding a strong relationship with him through worship and preaching. Seminary attenders usually touted counseling and social work as the "cutting edge of ministry" during the 1960s. While these are still seen as quite important, a more balanced understanding now recognizes that the power to accomplish these important ministries comes from something more basic—the Christ connection.

This trend has roots in another of Jesus' megatruths: *Concentrating your attention on Christ strengthens your ability to enter and experience God's kingdom in greater fullness.* A few examples from his teachings: "I am the vine, you are the branches" (John 15:5). "Again Jesus spoke to them, saying, 'I am the light of the world. Whoever follows me will never walk in darkness but will have the light of life'" (John 8:12). "All things have been handed over to me by my Father; and no one knows the Son except the Father, and no one knows the Father except the Son and anyone to whom the Son chooses to reveal him" (Matthew 11:27). "I have called you friends, because I have made known to you everything that I have heard from my Father" (John 15:15).

From this megatruth, early church leaders soon developed the concept of a "Trinity." While the word itself does not appear in the New Testament, it is definitely inferred there. Church leaders built this idea from Jesus' teachings about himself and the Holy Spirit. He had told them they could come to the new level of consciousness that he called the kingdom of God through focusing their minds on him and his words. He had said that after his earthly life was finished they would find this truth coming alive for them in even better ways through the power of the "Counselor" or Holy Spirit. They soon found Jesus' predictions coming true. Through worship, through preaching and teaching about him, and through the presence of the Holy Spirit, people still experienced his life-changing presence.

MEGATRUTH THREE

Concentrating your attention on Christ strengthens your ability to enter and experience God's kingdom in greater fullness.

The concepts of Holy Spirit and Trinity are difficult to explain because they involve trying to define the great mystery, God himself. As someone has observed, if we could define God, he would not be God. Most explanations have therefore been based on analogies that do not totally explain God's nature. But these word-picture comparisons do help us see a vague outline of what Jesus meant by this megatruth. Examples:

- Ice, water, and steam are all the same: H_2O. God is like the ice—firm like a great glacier, eternal, unchanging. Jesus is like the water—fluid and capable of taking on human form. The Holy Spirit is like vapor—unseen, yet powerful and capable of being everywhere at once.

- There is a sense in which a tree, the fruit that grows on it, and the seed in the fruit are "one." All are different manifestations of the same basic reality. God is the tree. Jesus is the fruit. The Holy Spirit is the seed of that fruit, living on long after the fruit has disappeared, re-producing again and again in other times and places.

- The same man can be a father (parent) and a husband (companion-friend) and a teacher (instructor). He doesn't do all these at the same time, but at different moments he takes on each of these roles. Being one of them does not keep him from being the other two. He is one person with different manifestations. From the earliest years of the church, the "threefold blessing" used in worship has expressed this same concept— "the grace of the Lord Jesus Christ, the love of God, and the fellowship of the Holy Spirit."

In the early eighteenth century, John Wesley saw Jesus' megatruth in action, and eventually experienced it person-ally, through his contact with the Moravians (a body of dis-senters from the Lutheran Church). In 1739, he began preaching "the witness of the Spirit" as a personal conscious-ness and started forming societies of those who accepted his teaching. He tried to remain loyal to the Church of England but in 1784 organized his "Methodists" in the United States into a separate church.

Pentecostalism, though not a single sect as much as an emphasis used by several denominations, leans heavily on this teaching of Jesus. These revivalistic groups, assemblies, movements, and churches are primarily concerned with relating individuals to Christ through the experience of the Holy Spirit in order to lead them into an experience of changed life. The modern charismatic movement, which began to attract adherents from many mainline denominations in the early 1960s—Catholic, Presbyterian, Methodist, Episcopal, Assembly of God, etc.—used this teaching as a major foundation stone of their "new" theology. This emphasis has influenced a renewal of evangelistic and didactic energy in all denominations. In 1781, William Herschel saw the planet Uranus through a telescope. Using accepted laws of planetary motion, he plotted its course. But Uranus behaved strangely. There had to be an unseen star causing its unusual movements. Another astronomer, Leverrier, worked out the location of the invisible star. Finally, with an improved lens, the German astronomer, Galle, actually saw Neptune, the planet which causes Uranus to behave as it does.

Across the centuries, people have known that there is an unseen presence in the universe. But they couldn't see it. Then came one who did see clearly. His words and actions pointed to something beyond himself, making it obvious that God is here. Those who looked closely at Christ saw God. And they still do.

Discovery Questions for Group Discussion

1. Read John 12:44–50. Jesus says that his words come from God. These teachings, along with those of the Old Testament, were major factors in the development of civil laws in England, Canada, and the U.S. List some examples of these laws.

2. Read John 10:1–42. Jesus says that he is one with God, the door of the sheep, and the good shepherd by which

people enter the kingdom. He is contrasting himself with those who try to enter the kingdom by other methods. Do you think people today sometimes try to enter the new level of consciousness that Jesus called the kingdom of God through other doors? If so, list some of these.

3. Read John 14:5–11. Jesus says he is the way, the truth, and the life by which people come to God. Do you think denominations sometimes set themselves and their teachings up as the way, the truth, and the life? Illustrate. How do you think we can avoid this tendency in our own denomination? our own local church?

4. Read John 14:15–27 and John 15:26. Jesus says that those who love him by concentrating on his words and commandments will receive his continuing presence through the Counselor, the Holy Spirit. Looking back over your life, have there been times when you feel you have personally experienced the truth of this text? Illustrate.

5. Read John 16:4–15. Jesus says that the Holy Spirit (Spirit of Truth) will replace his presence with the disciples and guide them into all truth in the same way he (Jesus) has done, while at the same time educating the world concerning sin, righteousness, and judgment. Illustrate ways in which you think this happens in churches today.

6. Read John 15:1–16. Jesus says that the disciples must concentrate on him in order to bear the fruit of the kingdom. List the most helpful ways by which you, personally, are able to maintain contact with Christ and thus be energized to do his work and will.

7. Do you feel contemporary churches have tended to neglect this megatruth? Illustrate.

8. Do you think some contemporary churches have carried this megatruth to an extreme? Illustrate.

9. What recommendations would you make to leaders of your own local church regarding this megatruth?

Additional Examples

Peter recognizes that Jesus is from God. (Matthew 16:13–18; Mark 8:27–30; and Luke 9:18–20)

Jesus helps people see that he is the Christ (anointed one) of God's kingdom. (Mark 12:35–37; Matthew 22:41–46; and Luke 20:39–44)

The disciples are told to listen to Jesus because he is the Son of God. (Matthew 17:1–9; Mark 9:2–10; and Luke 9:28–36)

Jesus tells the woman at the well that he is God's anointed one of the kingdom. (John 4:16–30)

Jesus says he is the Christ (anointed one) of the kingdom. (John 18:33–37; Mark 15:1–2; and Luke 22:14–20)

Jesus tries to help his critics see that his authority comes from God. (Matthew 21:23–27; Mark 11:27–33; and Luke 20:39–44)

The Jews seek to kill Jesus because he has identified himself as equal with God. (John 5:18–24)

Jesus says to the Pharisees that they should come to the kingdom through recognizing him as God, rather than seeking it through the scriptures or other people. (John 5:30–47)

Jesus proclaims through healing a blind man that he has come from God to help people see the kingdom. (John 9:1–41)

Jesus says he is the light from God and says that people can more easily believe this because he has the power to raise Lazarus from the dead. (John 11:1–44)

Jesus says that to believe in him is to do the work of God and that God has put his seal on him. (John 6:25–59)

Jesus says his words help people enter the kingdom. (John 6:60–65)

Jesus says his teachings come from God. (John 7:14–19)

Jesus says he has been sent by God to help people find the kingdom. (John 7:28–29, 33–34, 37–39)

Jesus says he is from God, and those who follow him will find the light of life. (John 8:12–20)

Jesus says that he is speaking the truth from God, his Father. (John 8:25–30, 38–50, 54–59)

A voice from heaven is identified by many in the crowd as an angel whose words indicate that Jesus comes from God. (John 12:28–31)

Jesus identifies himself as the light from God—the Christ. (John 12:34–36)

Jesus says the disciples are right to call him teacher and Lord. (John 13:13)

On Palm Sunday, the blind, lame, children, and others recognize that Jesus is part of God's kingdom. (Matthew 21:14–16; and Luke 19:36–40)

A woman performs a symbolic act that recognizes Jesus as the Christ—anointed one. (Matthew 26:6–13; Mark 14:3–9; Luke 7:36–50; and John 12:1–8)

Jesus eats a symbolic meal with the disciples in which he identifies himself with the completion of God's kingdom. (Matthew 26:26–29; Mark 14:22–25; and Luke 22:14–20)

Jesus predicts that Judas will betray him in order that people will know that he is from God. (John 13:18–19)

Jesus says anyone who receives him receives God. (John 13:20)

In a long prayer, Jesus says that the disciples now know that he and all his words, love, and actions are from God. (John 17:1–26)

4

Raising Your Insights

D. L. Moody said, "If you have so much business to attend to that you have no time to pray, depend upon it, you have more business on hand than God ever intended you should have."

Brain wave research is beginning to uncover physiological evidence for that opinion. The alpha wave of seven to fourteen cycles per second seems to produce more "brain energy" than the normal beta level of fourteen to twenty-one cycles per second. The alpha wave is produced when a person is tranquil and relaxed, with eyes closed, as in a state of prayer or meditation. The beta wave is present in normal consciousness states of physical activity, tension, and problem solving. We seem to have one set of senses at the beta level of mind, the normal conscious state. At the alpha level, we apparently have another set of senses that communicate in other ways. ESP and other forms of paranormal communication seem to occur in this way.

One researcher says, "Could it be that God is trying to communicate with us all the time but can only do so when we have our receivers tuned to alpha? If so, isn't that a good reason to turn on and tune in? If we had some suspicion that a one thousand dollar check might arrive in the morning mail, wouldn't we walk out to the mailbox?"

An Indiana woman says, "In these troubled times, it is easy to become depressed and full of anxiety. This needless worry usually carries over into our performance and family relations. If only we could realize that the Lord is knocking at our doors all the time, wanting to be invited to come in and share the burdens of our worry. In our prayer, he will ease our minds and give us peace so that we can get along with the important plan God has for us. God is always near and ready to embrace us with his love and encouragement. And that comes through prayer."

Gallup Polls repeatedly reveal that many Americans who don't attend church do pray daily. What other religious practice has so penetrated secular language and life? The Senate opens its sessions with prayer. Many secular celebrations, such as graduations, begin with a prayer. Many families pray before meals. Even the persons who don't practice

MEGATRUTH FOUR

Prayer strengthens your ability to enter God's kingdom and experience it more fully.

prayer usually say they ought to and admire those who do. Carlyle was surely right when he said that prayer is the native and deepest impulse of the human soul.

These perceptions and practices grow out of another of Jesus' megatruths: *Prayer strengthens your ability to enter God's kingdom and experience it more fully.* Examples: "Ask, and it will be given you; search, and you will find; knock, and the door will be opened for you" (Matthew 7:7). In the model prayer Jesus gave the disciples, he instructed them to pray for the kingdom to come (Matthew 6:10). The record shows that Jesus practiced prayer much more frequently than he discussed it. He prayed in the morning before his disciples had awakened. He prayed before he made important decisions. When his disciples were troubled and fearful, Jesus prayed for them. Because of his close friends' grief, Jesus prayed. He even prayed for those who drove nails through his hands. (Luke 9:28; 22:32, 45; Matthew 14:23; 26:39, 42, 44; and Mark 1:35 are samples of this pattern.)

The disciples asked Jesus to teach them how to pray (Luke 11:1–4 and Matthew 6:9–15). Nowhere else do we find a request for instructions in how to do something. They don't say, "Teach us how to preach." They don't say, "Tell us how to build a church." They don't say, "Show us how to perform miracles." Jesus' prayer life was so visibly the crux of his strength that the disciples felt impelled to ask how they could be empowered in the same manner.

The first rise of monasticism, generally attributed to Anthony about A.D. 320, largely depends on this megatruth. At that time, Anthony began to attract public attention. Thousands of followers soon emulated his lifestyle. Anthony lived alone for years in an Egyptian cave. His disciples, called "anchorites" from a word meaning "retirement," soon thronged the caves of upper Egypt.

Simon, called Stylites, meaning "of the pillar," achieved even greater fame through this teaching. After leaving a monastery in A.D. 423, he built several pillars, each higher than its predecessor. The final one, only four feet broad, rose sixty feet into the air. Simon lived on these successively rising pillars for thirty-seven years, and thousands imitated his life. Syria boasted many pillar-saints between the fifth and twelfth centuries.

This form of the faith did not, however, obtain followers in Europe—perhaps because of the climate. Pillar sitting is most uncomfortable in northern European winters. But the solitary life of the ascetic did lead to the establishment in Europe of monasteries, where work was united with prayer. This teaching of Jesus has also found broad reaffirmation in virtually every contemporary denomination through the prayer group movement that arose in the 1960s as a spin-off of the small group movement, which became popular in many congregations at that time.

Innumerable practical values of prayer have been cited by various Christians. Among these are:

Guidance. Robert E. Spear, the Christian layman for whom the library at Princeton Seminary is named, said, "You can do more than pray after you have prayed; but you cannot do more than pray until you have prayed."

Strength. E. Stanley Jones was once asked how he was able to carry on such an enormous travel, speaking, and writing schedule year after year across five continents. He answered that he always kept up his prayer life daily, so that he did not have to face life alone.

Courage. Studdert Kennedy was an English chaplain in World War I whose speaking and writing helped many. He said that true prayer doesn't just ask for permission to survive; it asks for the courage to endure.

Doubt. A Catholic layman says the worst kind of doubt is not related to points of religious doctrine. Rather, doubt strikes hardest when we discover that we are not strong enough or clever enough to make our dreams come true. "Doubt is the constant companion of imperfect man," he says, "and its only remedy is prayer."[+]

Stress. Dr. Robert Eliot, a cardiologist from Nebraska, gives two rules for dealing with stress: "Rule number one is, don't sweat the small stuff. Rule number two is, it's all small stuff. And if you can't fight and you can't flee, flow." Paul Robbins adds, "We cannot see all stuff as small stuff unless we view it from God's perspective. To see the problems and stresses of each day from his line of sight requires proximity to him. Prayer must flow through our lives constantly, washing away the dust of stress."[++]

Self-Discovery. From the beginning of cognitive time, people have sought to discover the hidden aspects that they knew were below the surface of their own self-perception. The earliest psychological testing had its beginning in prayer. The ancients knew that in relating to God they might be able to get in touch with a bit of the subconscious. Many people

---

[+]*National Catholic Reporter,* March 1, 1974.
[++]Paul D. Robbins, "From the Office of the Publisher." *Leadership,* Summer 1983, Volume 4, No. 3.

still report that prayer helps them to know themselves better than when they search their soul with reason alone.

Self-Improvement. The inner life is the last unconquered frontier. We have touched our toes to the moon and planted our feet on every earthly island. But the conquest of the inner life of personality, the remaking of the elements that we don't want there, is still a fertile, untouched frontier. And many people find the only way they can enter and possess it is through prayer.

Interpersonal Relations. Many people report that failing to pray regularly damages not just themselves but everyone who lives close to them. It increases their tension level, multiplies their "hard-to-get-along-with factor," and generally fouls up their relationships with people.

Health. Dr. Edward Aubert, a British physician for more than thirty years, says modern medicine has become too materialistic and treats people as if they were mechanical entities, instead of living souls. He told an audience at St. Paul's Anglican Church in Toronto that patients who receive the religious rite of laying on of hands while undergoing proper medical treatment "do very much better" than others. The spelling error on one church bulletin may be more truth than "typo": "Congregation be seated for medication."

A Sunday school teacher requested that members of her class write a definition of prayer. One student turned in this sentence: "Prayer is messages sent up at night and on Sunday when the rates are cheaper." We would be stronger people if we more often used this method to raise our insights at other times.

Discovery Questions for Group Discussion

1. Read Matthew 7:7–11 (also found in Luke 11:9–13). Jesus says that whatever we ask will be given. How, then, do you explain the fact that not all prayers are answered?

2. Read Luke 11:5–15. In this scripture passage, which occurs just before the "Lord's Prayer," Jesus links

persistent prayer with the giving of the Holy Spirit to those who ask. List some ways in which you feel God gives people the Holy Spirit.

3. Read Mark 11:20–25. In this text and many others in the New Testament, Jesus links the need to forgive people with the experience of prayer. Explain why you think he said that so frequently. Jesus says that believing is a prime requirement for receiving. Is that a good argument for or against prayer in schools, the U.S. Senate, and football games? Give reasons for your opinion.

4. Read Matthew 21:12–13 (also found in Mark 11:15–17; Luke 19:45–46; and John 2:13–17). Jesus accuses the religious leaders of diverting the primary purpose of the temple—prayer—into another use. List various ways by which you think contemporary churches are tempted to do that.

5. Jesus prayed on several occasions according to the gospel records. At what times of the day and in what ways have you found it most beneficial to pray?

6. Do you feel contemporary churches tend to neglect this megatruth? Illustrate.

7. Do you feel some contemporary churches carry this megatruth to extremes? Illustrate.

8. What recommendations do you have for leaders of your local church regarding this megatruth?

Additional Examples

Using a parable about an unrighteous judge who responds to *persistent* requests, Jesus urges persistent prayer for those who enter the kingdom. (Luke 18:1–8)

Jesus tells the disciples that if two of them agree on something to ask, God will give it to them. (Matthew 18:19–20)

Jesus tells the disciples that some kinds of demons can only be driven out by prayer. (Mark 9:28–29)

Jesus finds through prayer the strength to give to his life and tells the disciples to pray that they may avoid temptation. (Matthew 26:36–46; Mark 14:32–42; and Luke 22:39–46)

5

Fold, Spindle, and Mutilate Your Idols

Devil Anse Hatfield, more than seven feet tall, was the patriarch in a clan whose feud with the McCoy family is unparalleled in American history. From the last days of the Civil War in 1864 through 1921, several dozen members of these families murdered each other in the mountains of eastern Kentucky and West Virginia.

The end of the bloodshed began when the aging Devil Anse had several conversations with William Dyke Garrett, a well-known minister of Logan County, West Virginia, who had fought with the Logan Wildcats in the Civil War before taking up the ministry. From the time Devil Anse was baptized in the waters of Island Creek, his neighbors described him as "much changed." After that, he began trying to make reparations for some of the ravages inflicted on both families. Thus, a colorful but bloody era came to an end, succumbing finally to the quiet but powerful force of Christianity.

Devil Anse Hatfield illustrates another of the Carpenter's megatruths: *You are blocked from entering God's kingdom unless you turn away from self-centeredness.* Examples: "From that time Jesus began to proclaim, 'Repent, for the kingdom of heaven has come near'" (Matthew 4:17; also Mark 1:15). Jesus' metaphor about the narrow gate in Matthew 7:13–14 teaches that those who enter God's kingdom must make a clear choice between two alternatives. In Matthew 10:34–37, he indicates that for some persons this decision to enter God's kingdom will even necessitate the setting aside of important relationships with friends and family. In Luke 14:15–24, his parable of the great feast says that we enter the kingdom only by a desire to turn away from other life preoccupations. In Matthew 22:1–14, he tells a parable about a wedding dinner that can only be eaten by those who are willing to come and accept it.

The repentance Jesus urges is not just from *moral* badness, as we might easily conclude by listening to certain radio preachers. It involves something more basic than that—repentance from self-centeredness. A plane left New York in the late 1950s, bound for Europe. Not far from the coast, one of the engines caught fire and the aircraft turned back. One of the passengers seated on the right side of the plane observed the fire out the left window and continued to read his newspaper. A stewardess, noticing how calm he was in the midst of all the other frightened passengers, inquired about his complacent attitude. "Oh, I'm not worried," he said. "The fire is not on my side of the plane." To some degree, all earth's passengers are born with that kind of myopic self-centeredness, and they don't get over it until they repent.

MEGATRUTH FIVE

You are blocked from entering God's kingdom unless you turn away from self-centeredness.

Ralph Waldo Emerson described his times as the "age of the first person singular," but that description fits every age. Original sin is also continual and residual sin, keeping us focused on the self. At birth, people come into a state of conscious awareness. But Jesus points to a still higher level of consciousness. He warns that many people live out their lives looking without seeing, listening without hearing, experiencing without understanding. Those fortunate enough to awaken from their coma begin with a moment of insight that allows them to have clear "outsight." Jesus calls that moment of new birth "repentance." Preoccupation with self travels in many disguises, using a number of aliases. For some, it comes clothed in devotion to hard work. For others, the pursuit of pleasure, the seeking of money, the search for personal power, or even the effort to attain high religious standards is the shell underneath which the kernel of selfishness hides. In one of the old Tarzan movies, the plot revolves around a pagan god a group of explorers is seeking to find. Tarzan asks a native chieftain what he knows about this god—a four-faced creature named Tumbero. The chief replies with a gem of wisdom: "The world is full of private gods. I have not seen this one." That is as true in our civilized world as it was among primitive savages. People bow before an endless variety of private idols. The first and second commandments are still broken more than any of the others. Could that be the reason they are listed first?

But Jesus does not just ask people to repent *from* something. He asks them to repent toward something—the higher consciousness of the kingdom of God. One of the early feeder airlines that served small communities in Texas used the motto: "Rio Airlines—Your First Step to Everywhere!" That was their commercial way of saying that people who intended to fly to London or New Zealand from the great Dallas–Fort Worth International Airport must *begin* their journey on Rio. Jesus says repentance is the first step to everywhere in the kingdom. By that process, we move away from self-centeredness (false reality) toward God-centeredness (true reality). Only from that point can we get in touch with the true First Person Singular—God—and thereby arrive at a perspective that includes the second and third person plural.

Many monastic groups stressed this teaching (the natural corollary of Megatruth Number Seventeen regarding the need for self-giving). Sects and movements that build their theology and life around Megatruth Number Seventeen tend also to stress the need to repent of self-centeredness. But instead of expressing it in forceful concrete doctrines, they usually hold it in the background as a silent assumption. Denominations that view salvation (wholeness) as an escape from eternal fires of hell (usually by stressing Megatruth Number Nineteen) also tend to lay heavy emphasis on this repentance theme.

Death is not our biggest danger. We should far more fear the fate of never deciding to begin living.

Discovery Questions for Group Discussion

1. Read Luke 15:1–2 and Luke 15:11–32. Do you feel your denomination emphasizes the concept of repentance found in the text above too much or too little? Give reasons for your opinion.

2. Read Matthew 21:28–32. Jesus says the kingdom can come to "nonreligious outsiders" who repent while the ritually pure, religious Jews who do not repent can miss it. Have you known individuals in these two categories to whom that seems to have happened?

3. Read Luke 13:1–5. Jesus does not so much speak of repenting from evil deeds as of repenting from a false religion that misses the reality of God. List some of the ways you feel people in your denomination need to hear that message. Do you think this relates in any way to the radical membership declines of several denominations since 1960?

4. Read Matthew 8:18–22. List some of the things you feel contemporary people have to leave behind in order to enter the kingdom.

5. Read Mark 9:43–48. Jesus dramatizes with literary hyperbole the need to seek God's kingdom first rather than

making it a secondary matter. Thinking back over your own life, are you willing to name some of the "other kingdoms" that you feel have tended to distract you from seeking his kingdom?

6. When you first became a Christian, do you remember experiencing a feeling of repentance? Did you feel you were repenting away from something bad or toward something good?

7. What recommendations do you have for leaders of your local church regarding this megatruth? for your denomination?

6

The Greatest Religious Temptation

Humpty Dumpty is not alone. The Christian world now boasts 2,400 different denominational families. More than 250 exist in the U.S. alone, with twenty-eight denominations containing more than one-half million members each. Twenty-seven others contain between 100,000 and 500,000 members. All the king's horses and all the king's men have been insufficient to put the church back together again.

Denominations have not, of course, been all bad. They penetrate the culture better than a single monolithic church. In England, 12 percent of the population attends worship on an average Sunday morning. In the U.S., that figure stands at 38 percent. Different kinds of people respond to the different denominational interpretations of Jesus' message. More options bring larger numbers of responses. We should, therefore, not be too hasty in condemning this plethora of name brands. But New Testament teachings about humility do force us to condemn the extreme pride and self-righteousness some of them exhibit.

God and his truth cannot be captured in a denominational box. When our ideologies become our idolatries, we break the second commandment and disregard one of Jesus' megatruths: *Taking pride in your religious achievements makes it difficult to enter God's kingdom.* Examples: "Whoever becomes humble like this child is the greatest in the kingdom of heaven" (Matthew 18:4). In other texts, Jesus elaborates on the need for erasing religious pride and becoming like children in order to enter the kingdom (Mark 9:33–37 and Luke 9:46–48). In Matthew 19:13–15, he says children have qualities of humility that allow them to enter the kingdom more easily. In Matthew 23:1–12, the perils of religious pride are contrasted to the virtue of religious humility. He says in Matthew 5:3 and Luke 6:20 that those who feel a sense of spiritual poverty find God-consciousness more easily because they aren't blocked by their religious pride. In Matthew 6:16–18, he warns against the religious pride that so easily arises from public displays of fasting. In Matthew 6:1–8, he says we should avoid ostentation in prayers and charities.

Few denominations built their beginnings on this megatruth. New movements cannot be born unless the leaders have strong convictions about the rightness of their suggested reforms. The courage needed for that kind of leadership seldom contains an oversupply of humility. The Quakers and some of the Roman Catholic orders led by people like Saint Francis of Assisi have made excellent attempts at combining humility with spiritual renewal. Christian history repeatedly teaches, however, that our magnetic drift toward pride and self-righteousness is always stronger than the pull toward humility.

The Old Order Amish of Pennsylvania wear uniform clothing with hooks instead of buttons in order to avoid prideful display. For many of them, that practice is a genuine act of humility. But even here, temptation lurks close at hand. These overt acts of humility can so easily become a prideful way of saying: "We are better than other people.

MEGATRUTH SIX

Taking pride in your religious achievements makes it difficult to enter God's kingdom.

Look how humble we are!" Members of every denomination face the same danger. Even the ecumenical groups that continually point to their tolerance of other churches can do this as a way of feeling superior to other, more dogmatic Christians.

Some religious people are always letting off steam. How can we avoid this tendency toward self-righteousness? Jesus directs us to become like a child again, recognizing our lack of perfection and our dependence on God.

Discovery Questions for Group Discussion

1. Read Luke 18:9–14. Jesus says that those who exalt themselves will be humbled and vice versa. Give some examples from contemporary society or your own life that seem to prove the truth of that teaching. Does other evidence seem to point in the opposite direction?

2. Read Matthew 18:1–4 (also found in Mark 10:14 and Luke 18:16–17). Reflecting on this text, try to recall the most humble Christian you ever knew. Describe him or her. In what ways did his or her character contain the childlike qualities which Jesus says those who enter the kingdom must have?

3. Read Matthew 23:1–12 (also found in Mark 12:38–40 and Luke 20:45–47). Jesus warns against the kind of religious pride that seeks titles, places of honor, and symbolic garments. This is always a danger in any type of religion— that the outer symbols subtly replace the inner spirit. Looking back over the last few years, what similar dangers do you think Christians need to guard against today?

4. Read Matthew 6:1–8. Using examples of giving money and praying, Jesus warns that we should beware of parading our piety before other people. If you were asked to give advice to national political leaders, ministers,

and local laypersons regarding this truth, what would you say to each group?

5. Read Luke 7:29–35 (also found in Matthew 11:16–19). The religious leaders were too proud to listen to the truth from Jesus and John the Baptist. Do you think any contemporary religious or political situations seem similar—with leaders refusing to hear the truth because it comes from humble sources?

6. Read Matthew 5:5. Many scholars think the contemporary English word "meek" may not convey the true meaning of Jesus' statement. What do you think Jesus meant by this statement?

7. Do you think some contemporary churches have carried the truth of Jesus' teaching about humility to extremes? Illustrate.

8. What recommendations do you have for leaders of your local church regarding this megatruth? for leaders of your denomination?

Additional Examples

In the temptations which precede the beginning of his ministry, Jesus rejects the option of religious showmanship. (Matthew 4:7 and Luke 4:12)

Jesus says religious people who are proud that they have no guilt are by that pride declaring their own guilt. (John 9:40–41)

With a parable about how guests are seated at a banquet, Jesus says those with great pride will be humbled and those with humility will be honored. (Luke 14:7–11)

Following the healing of the blind man, Jesus says those who see the world through eyes filled with religious pride are actually blind and those who view it through eyes of humility will see. (John 9:35–39)

7

Putting Second Things First Gets Results

The ancient Spartans had no trouble remembering that wealth is a burden. They minted their money in heavy iron disks rather than small silver coins. Even in paper form, cash can be hard to carry. John D. Rockefeller said, "I have learned that I cannot give an individual substantial amounts of money without hurting him." The prodigal son in Jesus' famous parable experienced that stress. When he got his inheritance, he caught a bad case of self-sufficiency. With all that money, who needs God and family?

A thousand years earlier, Moses saw the same problem. Leading his band of refugees into a new land, he said: "Take care....When you have eaten your fill and have built fine houses and live in them, and when your herds and flocks have multiplied, and your silver and gold is multiplied, and all that you have is multiplied, then do not exalt yourself, forgetting the LORD your God, who brought you out of the land of Egypt, out of the house of slavery" (Deuteronomy 8:11–14).

Moses' warning didn't take. When they had matured from an oppressed tribe of slaves into a prosperous commercial nation, they forgot. Agur, living in those good new days, looked around at the spiritual decline and prayed, "...give me neither poverty nor riches;...or I shall be full, and deny you, and say, 'Who is the LORD?'" (Proverbs 30:8–9). In want, we ask God to help. In plenty, we tend toward preoccupation with possessions. Money can fill up the heart until little space remains for the spiritual.

This is not, however, a hazard of the rich alone. Middle-income and poor people can also become preoccupied with money—the lack of it and how to get more of it. That, too, can block out the presence of God.

Observing this common human tendency to put second things first, Jesus devoted much teaching time to another megatruth: *Financial wealth makes it more difficult for you to enter God's kingdom because your money brings a false sense of power that distracts you from seeking something better.* Examples: "It is easier for a camel to go through the eye of a needle than for someone who is rich to enter the kingdom of God" (Mark 10:25). In Matthew 6:19–34, Jesus urges us to seek first God's kingdom, rather than riches, since putting something else at first priority can block us from our God relationship. In Matthew 19:16–26, Jesus tells a wealthy young man to sell all he has because it is blocking him from entering God's kingdom. In Luke 6:20, Jesus says that the poor are happy because they are not distracted by the false god of wealth. In Luke 16:1–13, the story of a rich man and his employee urges the wise use of money for spiritual purposes.

MEGATRUTH SEVEN

Financial wealth makes it more difficult for you to enter God's kingdom because your money brings a false sense of power that distracts you from seeking something better.

A motorist was fascinated by the construction of a beautiful skyscraper—so fascinated that he ran off the street and hit a light post. The new building was not intrinsically bad. It was not the building but his misplaced preoccupation that caused the crash. That is how Jesus described money. Don't put it first, his Sermon on the Mount says, "Strive first for the kingdom of God and his righteousness, and all these things will be given to you as well" (Matthew 6:33).

Jesus had faced the same temptation. The forty-day wilderness experience was a struggle for perspective and priorities. Why not despiritualize the kingdom? Couldn't God be communicated best by materialistic miracles like feeding the hungry? Jesus replied with words out of Deuteronomy, "One does not live by bread alone, but by every word that comes from the mouth of God" (Matthew 4:4). Going to first base gets you to second base. Running for second base first gets you called out.

Human attention has limited capacity. Preoccupation with one priority limits our ability to concentrate on another. That is what Jesus said to the rich young ruler who came wanting to be a disciple: "If you wish to be perfect, go, sell your possessions, and give the money to the poor" (Matthew 19:21). Jesus did not prescribe that remedy for everyone. This was the only person to whom he gave such a stern command. And he did not do so because money is bad. He saw that the man was so hooked on money he couldn't hook onto anything else. The man went away sorrowful. His life was too full of the small god. Full house, no room left in the inn, and he didn't have the courage to turn it out.

The rich young ruler is one of the persons Jesus describes in the parable of the seed. Some fall among thistles. These people hear the message, but it comes in second—behind economic struggle and the lure of getting rich (Matthew 13:22). Hold a gold Krugerrand at arm's length and you can see the world around it. Hold it against your eye and it blocks your vision. The coin isn't intrinsically bad, no matter where you hold it. But putting it first is an expensive decision. No amount of money can buy back what you lose.

God said through Moses: "You shall not make gods of silver alongside me, nor shall you make for yourselves gods of gold" (Exodus 20:23). That injunction goes far deeper than pagan idol worship. It applies to modern idol worship, too.

And the results are the same—separation from God and the life-giving level of consciousness he invites us to enter. The Benedictines, founded by Saint Benedict in A.D. 529, built their popular movement on this megatruth. They grew into the largest of the monastic communities. Poverty or the possession of zero property by the monks and nuns was a basic requirement.

Some of the radical Christian youth movements of the turbulent 1960s preached the same idea. They seldom practiced it for long periods, however. For some of them, poverty was a *perversion* of Jesus' megatruth. They didn't reject wealth in favor of God; they rejected both. Rather than putting first things first and second things second, they put neither anyplace. Independence and freedom from authority became their highest priority. Money is not the only preoccupation that can make us poor.

Mrs. Green was the conservative treasurer of a small country church. "How much will it cost?" she always asked regarding every new idea in church life. After thirty years of her raising that question, everyone in the small community was aware of her priority. One day Mrs. Green telephoned the small town fire department and asked the chief, "How much would it cost to have a fire truck come out to Bethel Church?"

He quoted her a general figure and added that this would depend on several factors. After they talked a few minutes, he got suspicious. "Say," he asked, "would Bethel Church by any chance be on fire right now?"

"Yes, it is," she replied.

Mrs. Green was putting second things first. When we do that with our lives, the result is a poverty no amount of money can cure.

Discovery Questions for Group Discussion

1. Read Matthew 19:16–26 (also found in Luke 18:18–27 and Mark 10:17–27). Jesus says it is difficult, though not

impossible, for wealthy persons to enter the new level of consciousness that he calls the kingdom of God. Why do you think this is true? Why is it more difficult for these persons than for others?

2. Read Mark 12:13–17. Jesus warns that the love of accumulating money and what it can buy can keep people out of God's kingdom. In what ways do you think we can combat this tendency in ourselves?

3. Read Matthew 6:19–24. Jesus uses the term "kingdom of heaven" interchangeably with "kingdom of God" in most of his teachings. What do you think he means by that term here? In what ways do you think it is possible to lay up treasure in heaven?

4. Read Luke 16:1–13. This parable has been one of the most difficult for scholars to interpret. Many feel Jesus is urging a wise use of money for spiritual purposes, like the giving of alms. This interpretation would be consistent with the many other teachings about money and helping the poor found in Luke's Gospel. The parable could, however, be a satire about the folly of relating to money instead of God. What do you think the parable means?

5. Jesus says in Matthew 6:19–24 that we cannot serve God and money, too. Yet, money is a necessity for persons of every income level. In what ways can we handle this dilemma?

6. Do you think giving money to support the work of churches helps us cope with the tendency money has to control our lives?

7. Should our church teach more of Jesus' ideas about money, or less? Why?

8. Do you think some denominations have carried this megatruth to extremes? Illustrate.

9. What advice would you give leaders of our denomination regarding this megatruth?

Additional Examples

Jesus says in the parable of soils that wealth can choke out our response to God-consciousness. (Matthew 13:22; Mark 4:18–19; and Luke 8:14)

Jesus says accumulating many possessions will not bring us into the kingdom. (Mark 8:36–37 and Luke 9:25–26)

Jesus urges the disciples to concentrate on self-giving rather than on their possessions. (Luke 12:32–34)

8

Dessert Before Dinner

According to George Gallup, 12 percent of American adults are "highly spiritually committed" and live what they would describe as a "devout life." Gallup says the members of this group are "a breed apart from the rest of the populace in at least four ways: They are happier, their families are stronger, they are tolerant of people of different races and religions, and they are community-minded."[+]

Researchers from Johns Hopkins found that a lifetime of regular church attendance significantly reduced cardiovascular diseases in older adults. They also discovered that non-attendees had higher mortality rates for such other diseases as cirrhosis of the liver, emphysema, arteriosclerosis, and other cardiovascular diseases, as well as suicide. Blood pressure, another key factor in cardiovascular health, is also significantly reduced by regular church attendance.[++]

A widely circulated statistical report of unknown origin apparently pulled those and other data together to claim that

---

[+]George Gallup, 166th Meeting of the American Bible Society. June 4, 1982, issue of *The National Christian Reporter*.

[++]George W. Comstock and Kay B. Partridge: "Church attendance and health." *Journal of Chronic Disease*, Vol. 25, 1972, pp. 665–672.

persons who regularly attend church (a) live 5.7 years longer than non-attenders, (b) are 60 percent less likely to have a heart attack, and (c) are 55 percent less likely to have a one-car accident.

Bob Harrington, the famous "pastor of Bourbon Street" in New Orleans, said during a Dallas television interview that his cuff links are engraved with a scriptural paraphrase of 3 John 1:2: "It is the will of God that you prosper and be in good health." Harrington said he believes that entering God's kingdom brings financial rewards.[+] He is not alone in these views. Many among the "new religious right" have taken up the abundant life concept and pushed it back to, and perhaps beyond, similar concepts found among Old Testament Hebrews of three thousand years ago.

Research supports these views. Regular church attendance helps young people in particular to escape the poverty of inner-city life. For the nation as a whole, people who regularly go to church as youth earn about eleven thousand dollars more in annual income by their early thirties, no matter whether they come from intact or broken families (another key influence).[++]

While sincere Christians can make strong arguments both for and against the logic and accuracy of such research and opinion, each is to some degree consistent with another of Jesus' megatruths: *Though self-concern is not your goal, you receive rich rewards by entering God's kingdom.* Examples: "Blessed rather are those who hear the word of God and obey it!" (Luke 11:28). In Matthew 5:1–12, Jesus lists among the Beatitudes numerous rewards for those who enter the kingdom. In Mark 8:34–35, he says that those who take up their cross of sacrifice will be rewarded. In Luke 14:7–11, he says that those who sit humbly at the lowest places shall be exalted. In Mark 10:29–31, he notes that the last shall be first. In Matthew 5:10, he implies that persecuted disciples find much

---

[+]Dallas TV interview, November 1979.

[++]*Update,* edited by Nicholas D. van Dyck, fall 1996, "The Impact of Religious Practice on Social Stability" by Patrick F. Fagan, pp. 1–8.

happiness and personal satisfaction in knowing that they are doing God's will. In Matthew 5:11–12, he promises the disciples that he will reward them by personally commending them to God. In Mark 9:41, he promises rewards for those who serve well. In Matthew 11:29, he borrows "the yoke of the law" phrase from the rabbis in order to say that those who take up his yoke will find rest for their souls. In Matthew 19:27–30, he indicates that entering the kingdom is synonymous with inheriting eternal life and promises hundredfold rewards to those who have followed him at great personal sacrifice. In Matthew 6:19–20, he speaks of rewards laid up in heaven. In Luke 20:34–38, he says that those who attain the resurrection will become like angels.

The theology (considered a paratheology by some) of "rational positivism" that pervaded the preaching of many denominations following World War II leaned heavily on this teaching.

MEGATRUTH EIGHT

Though self-concern is not your goal, you receive rich rewards by entering God's kingdom.

Rather than emphasizing streets paved with gold, it stressed rewards like success, peace of mind, courage, and a richer personal life. This popular viewpoint did not result in the formation of a new sect, but it did spawn a new school of popular thought among pastors and members of several religious bodies.

It is not difficult to find personal testimonies that substantiate popular interpretations of this megatruth. A judicatory official and his wife lost all their lifetime belongings in a fire that wiped out their Houston, Texas, apartment only a few months prior to retirement. This painful experience came shortly after some other tragic personal losses had struck friends and family members. Yet, in writing to his constituency, the church official said, "There is an ancient story from the early days of the Church that tells of a Roman emperor who sent a runner to see how the Christians who were awaiting death in the arena were acting. The messenger returned and reported, 'Sire, they are singing!' We share a faith that enables us to sing, no matter what we face. Paul was right when he said, 'For I am convinced that neither death, nor life…nor anything else in all creation, will be able to separate us from the love of God in Christ Jesus our Lord' (Romans 8:38–39)."

The Old Testament Hebrews quite literally believed that "the hand of our God is gracious to all who seek him, but his power and his wrath are against all who forsake him" (Ezra 8:22). But Jesus added a new dimension. He said that even when bad things happen to good people, they can still feel strong if they have a strong relationship with God. The Jews said God gives you better circumstances. Jesus said God also gives you the better attitudes and feelings which allow you to transcend your bad circumstances.

An apartment complex in Ohio is called "Good Life Apartments." A large billboard in a western city says, "Happiness is a home in Hunsley Hills." These examples of good advertising are not examples of good logic. Happiness is not a state of geography; happiness is a state of mind—a state of mind rarely produced by where we live. Happiness is produced mostly by how we *think*.

Jesus says in another megatruth that we can live right through death (see chapter 12). But that is not his only good news. He also says we can live before death. We do not have to wait for pie in the sky by and by. We can have our dessert before dinner—providing we take the initiative to sit down at the table of God-consciousness.

In several laboratories across the country, dental researchers are working on an amazing new tooth decay preventative—a kiss. Helpful bacteria in the human mouth, when processing sugar from food, produce an acid which attacks tooth enamel. But a new strain of bacteria has been discovered. It not only does not produce acid; it acts like a street sweeper in discouraging harmful bacteria from sticking to teeth surfaces. Experiments in laboratory animals point toward the time when a kiss from mom can transfer enough protective bacteria to prevent tooth decay.[+] Likewise, Jesus says people can find immunity from many of life's greatest distresses by contact with a new level of consciousness.

A van parked in a restaurant parking lot said on its side "Abundant Life Church." Those adjectives may not characterize everyone who enters that particular church building, but Jesus says they describe persons who enter the kingdom.

Discovery Questions for Group Discussion

1. Read Matthew 10:39 and Matthew 16:25 (also found in Luke 9:24 and Mark 8:35). What do you think Jesus means by his statement?

2. Read Matthew 10:40–42 (also found in Luke 10:16). Jesus says that anyone who helps him or one of his disciples will be rewarded. How do you think his statement applies in contemporary society?

3. Read Matthew 23:11–12. Jesus says that those who serve others and show humility in their religious practices will be rewarded. Can you give illustrations of how that principle seems to work in contemporary churches? in contemporary society?

4. Read John 10:9–10. Jesus says that those who follow him will find abundant life. In what ways do you feel that this statement has come true in your personal life?

5. Read Luke 11:27–28. When Jesus says that those who hear and keep the Word of God will be blessed, he is emphasizing the living of his megatruths rather than the mere knowing or discussing of them. Can you give some examples from community life or church life of

---

[+] First Christian Church Newsletter (mimeo), Liberal, Kansas, article by John Loucks, pastor, January 9, 1984.

our tendency to substitute the discussing of faith for the living of it?

6. Read Matthew 20:1–16. Jesus seems to say that we are rewarded for entering the kingdom, no matter when or how we enter and even though we do not come in through traditional religious avenues. Do you think that means we can enter God-consciousness without affiliating with a church?

7. Read Mark 9:38–41 (also found in Luke 9:49–50). Jesus says all persons who do good work in his name will be rewarded, even though they do not seem to be like us. Do you think the acceptance of this truth has been the root cause of vastly improved relationships among denominations in America during the last thirty years, or has this come about through other means? Give reasons for your opinions.

8. Read Matthew 19:27–30 (also found in Mark 10:29–31 and Luke 18:28–30; 22:28–30). Jesus says his followers will be rewarded one hundredfold and will receive eternal life at the final coming of the kingdom. Do you think some denominations have carried this teaching to extremes?

9. Read John 3:18. Jesus says that those who believe in him will have eternal life. Do you think preaching and teaching in our church emphasizes this megatruth too much? too little? Why?

10. What advice would you give leaders of your church regarding this megatruth?

Additional Examples

Jesus says in the parable about wheat and weeds that the wheat will be gathered into barns at the harvest. (Matthew 13:30, 43)

Jesus says the kingdom grows into a great harvest through a power we cannot see or understand. (Mark 4:26–29)

Paul quotes Jesus as saying it is more blessed to give than to receive. (Acts 20:35)

Using the parable of an unrighteous judge, Jesus says those who persistently seek to enter the kingdom will be rewarded at the end time when Christ comes. (Luke 18:1–8)

Jesus says those who have done good will have eternal life. (John 5:29)

Jesus says those who acknowledge him before men will be rewarded. (Matthew 10:32; Luke 12:8; and Mark 13:13)

Jesus says those who take no offense at him are blessed. (Matthew 11:6 and Luke 7:23)

Jesus says whoever does the will of his Father is his brother and sister. (Matthew 12:46–50; Mark 3:31–34; and Luke 8:19–21)

Jesus tells the Jews that if they continue in his Word they will know the truth and be free from the bondage of sin and their meaningless religious traditions. (John 8:31–37)

Jesus says people who recognize, serve, and follow him will be honored by God. (John 12:25–26)

Jesus says those who follow him will find the light of life. (John 8:12–20)

Jesus says those who abide in him bear much fruit. (John 15:5)

Jesus says whoever gives one of his disciples a cup of water will be rewarded. (Matthew 10:42; 18:5 and Mark 9:36–37, 41)

Jesus says those who are least in the kingdom are greater than John the Baptist, though no one who has been born is greater than him. (Matthew 11:11 and Luke 7:28)

Jesus tells the Samaritan woman at the well that those who believe in him will find eternal life. (John 4:7–15)

Jesus tells the Jews that those who believe in him will have eternal life. (John 5:21, 24)

Jesus says to those who seek rewards for being his disciples that it is God alone who grants rewards to those who enter the kingdom. (Matthew 20:23–24)

Jesus says the thief on the cross beside him will enter Paradise that day. (Luke 23:39–43)

Jesus says those who believe in him will find eternal life. (John 3:18)

Jesus promises blessings to those who, unlike Thomas, believe in him without having seen him alive following the resurrection. (John 20:29)

9

The Ultimate Security

Some safe things look dangerous. Some dangerous things look safe. During a recent year, 8.1 million scheduled commercial airplanes left the ground in the United States. Only two of these flights ended in fatal accidents. That makes trusting an unseen pilot to ride the wind at 35,000 feet thirty times safer than steering your own car on the ground. But a white-knuckled passenger, tensed up during a first flight, usually misses the significance of these comforting statistics. Security is sometimes hard to see, even when you are sitting in the middle of it.

The relaxed feeling level of a seasoned air traveler making the 400th trip is similar to what Jesus described in another megatruth: *Entering God's kingdom gives you a sense of security that comes from believing your personal needs will be taken care of.* Examples: "Therefore do not worry, saying, 'What will we eat?' or 'What will we drink?' or 'What will we wear?' For it is the Gentiles who strive for all these things; and indeed your heavenly Father knows that you need all these things. But strive first for the kingdom of God and his righteousness, and all these things will be given to you as well" (Matthew 6:31–33). In Matthew 10:5–13, he promises the twelve apostles special providence as he sends them out; they therefore do not need to take money or food with them. In Matthew 10:29–31, he says, "Are not two sparrows sold for a penny? Yet not one of them will fall to the ground apart from your Father. And even the hairs of your head are all counted. So do not be afraid; you are of more value than many sparrows."

Jesus was a living parable of this megatruth. He attacked each part of his tough assignment trustfully. Often in danger, he *lived out* the kind of life Henry Ford once recommended when someone asked him if he ever worried. "No, with God in charge, I believe everything will work out for the best in the end. So what is there to worry about?"

Jesus was not the first or last to teach this axiom. Hallways of the biblical record before and beyond him reverberate with the promise of ultimate security in the midst of the dangerous situations that accompany the experience of being alive:

"Do not fret—it leads only to evil" (Psalm 37:8). "And my God will fully satisfy every need of yours according to his riches in glory in Christ Jesus" (Philippians 4:19). Someone has said that a form of the phrase "fear not" appears in scripture 365 times— one for every day of the year. Whether this is precisely true may be debated, but it does drive home two often-repeated scriptural teachings: the eternal presence of insecurity in human existence, and the feelings of security available to cope with that condition.

MEGATRUTH NINE

Entering God's kingdom gives you a sense of security that comes from believing your personal needs will be taken care of.

A pastor summarized both Jesus' megatruth and the entire biblical record on this subject when he explained the meaning of the Hebrew word "shalom" to his people. "This word of greeting and closing is far more rich in meaning than 'hello' or 'goodbye' or 'how are you' or 'sincerely yours.' The word means a peaceful well-being, in which life is lived in harmony with the self, with others, with the environment, and with God. *That well-being begins and ends, not with a struggle for peace within the self, as many modern thinkers preach today, but with a relationship to God."*+

This megatruth is highly visible in contemporary religious life. Robert Schuller of The Crystal Cathedral, Garden Grove, California, beams it at several million persons in his national TV congregation with great persuasive power each Sunday morning. He blends optimism and Christian faith in a slightly different way than Norman Vincent Peale did three decades earlier. The theology of Christian success, considered spurious by some theologians in both that generation and this, has been reshaped by adding a theology of security.

Contemporary charismatic groups also lean heavily on Jesus' teaching about the ultimate security. Though this is certainly not their only emphasis, the tremendous emotional insecurity felt by many in our society is undoubtedly one of the reasons why 10 percent of religious adherents in the U.S. now classify themselves with a charismatic theological position.

In spite of its prevalence in both the biblical record and contemporary Christian preaching, most people find this megatruth more difficult to live than to hear and discuss. Last year, Americans consumed more than 25,000 tons of aspirin—many of which are used to treat stress-related pains in the head. We are fearful about our difficulties, fearful about the circumstances in which we must live, the tasks we attempt, and the unknown future we have yet to meet.

Humankind is *born* with a great sense of security. A child's relationship with his mother is one of total confidence. But we soon lose that as we mature into our own personhood. This is one of the reasons Jesus says we must be born again. We have to decide whether we will depend on a positive Person for the security which no set of circumstances can provide.

+*The Family Weekly*, July 22, 1984.

We keep hoping to achieve security by altering our circumstances. "If I could pass my exams.... If I had more money.... If I could move to a better neighborhood...." But did you ever meet a person who found a lasting sense of security by graduating to a new set of surroundings? No, security does not come from what is around us but from what is inside us. That is why Jesus urged us to seek a new consciousness rather than new circumstances. He did not completely spiritualize his teachings by saying material life is unimportant. But in his efforts to heal and help and feed, he never confused anyone about where the real kingdom is.

As part of an art contest, several painters produced pictures on the theme of "perfect peace." The two finalists had radically contrasting entries. One oil depicted a quiet lake in the mountains. The other showed a birch tree branch above a thundering waterfall. In a fork of the limb, only a short distance from the spray, sat a robin in her nest. The latter picture is closest to what Jesus painted—not life with stress subtracted but peace despite potential danger.

A census taker stopped at a modest house. Interviewing the weary mother of several children, he asked, "How many children do you have?"

"Well," she began, "There is Johnny and Mary..."

"No, no," the canvasser interrupted impatiently. "I don't want their names—just their number."

She replied indignantly, "They don't have numbers. They all have names." Jesus said those who enter the new level of consciousness can count on that same security. God knows our names. The hairs of our heads are numbered. Even when a sparrow falls, God sees and cares.

In his excellent book *The Preaching Event*, John Claypool has translated this megatruth into clear terms by reminding us that in "transactional analysis" language the spectrum of feelings most people move along goes from "I'm not okay" to "You're not okay" to "We're not okay" to "They're not okay" to "It's not okay." Claypool says that if we can finally see our Ultimate Source as positive rather than negative, someone to be trusted and collaborated with, our feelings can begin to move in the opposite direction: "I'm okay. You're okay. We're okay. They're okay. It's okay." If that happened to us, he says, "we would be able to feel differently, because the connection at the basis of our being would be made whole again, and the delight that God wanted us to know from the beginning would start to flow again."[+]

But most people have difficulty making that connection. Driving north out of Plainview, Texas, on a farm-to-market road, a motorist encountered a sign that said "Eight miles to Providence." Realizing he had not known there was such a place as Providence, Texas, he reflected that most people are far more than eight miles from God's Providence. They do not have an operational belief in that kind of security. They believe in self-help (God helps those who help themselves), but they do not really believe in God's help. And this subtle form of atheism robs them of the security Jesus said we all can step into.

During the midst of the Great Depression of the 1930s, a poverty-burdened older woman approached the front desk of an insurance office in Minneapolis. She wanted to know if she could stop making payments on the yellowed policy clutched in her farm-weathered fingers. The clerk gave it a perfunctory glance, then studied it with intent amazement. "This is quite valuable," he said. "I would not advise you to stop paying the premiums now, after all these years. Have you talked with your husband about this?"

"No," she said. "He has been dead for three years."

"What!" exclaimed the clerk. "But this is a policy on his life—a $300,000 policy."

Soon, the company had paid the benefits and refunded the three years of overpaid premiums. She now began to experience the financial security that she had had all the time but had not known about. Jesus said that happens when you

---

[+]John R. Claypool, *The Preaching Event* (Waco: Word Books, Inc., 1980), p. 5.

and I decide to walk into the kingdom. We find the feeling of security that was ours all the time.

Life is only secure when we risk it totally by putting it in God's hands. Security is not the absence of danger but the presence of God.

Discovery Questions for Group Discussion

1. Read Matthew 6:25–34 (also found in Luke 12:22–31). Have you known of Christians who seemed to take Jesus' promise of security to extremes? Illustrate. Have you known of Christians who seemed to go to the other extreme and live as if this megatruth did not exist? Illustrate. If you had to say that you, personally, are like the people in one of these two groups, which would most nearly describe you?

2. Read Matthew 10:5–13 (also found in Mark 6:8–10 and Luke 9:34; 10:3–9). Jesus sends out the twelve and assures them that their needs will be cared for. Do you think those statements have any application to people in contemporary churches?

3. Read Matthew 10:19–20 (also found in Mark 13:11 and Luke 12:11–12; 21:13–15). Jesus promises the disciples that God will give them words to speak at the times when they are brought under stress and fear because of their commitment to his kingdom. Have you ever had any experiences in which you felt that came true? Describe them.

4. Read John 14:27. Jesus promises his disciples a special kind of peace. Have you ever had a stressful life experience in the midst of which you felt a great peace and security settling over your mind in spite of the frightening circumstances? What suggestions would you make to other people who are seeking that experience of peace?

5. Have there been times in your life when you seemed to experience a sense of God's security more than at other times? What else was happening in your life during those times? Do you feel you were more nearly "seeking his kingdom" during those times?

6. Do you think some denominations or television preachers seem to emphasize this megatruth? Illustrate.

7. Do you think people in our period of history have a greater or lesser need of this megatruth than people earlier in this century? Why?

8. Would you, personally, like to hear more, about the same, or less of this megatruth from the pulpit of your church? Why?

Additional Examples

Jesus tells Martha not to be anxious but to seek instead his teachings about the kingdom. (Luke 10:38–42)

Jesus teaches his disciples to pray for their daily bread. (Matthew 6:11 and Luke 11:3)

Jesus says those who mourn will become happy. (Matthew 5:4 and Luke 6:21)

Jesus promises protection from persecutors. (Matthew 10:26–33 and Luke 12:1–7)

Jesus says that those who endure to the end will be saved. (Matthew 10:22)

Jesus says that even though the disciples are scattered after his death, they will have peace. (John 16:29–33)

Jesus appears to Paul and tells him not to be afraid to speak and teach about him in Corinth. (Acts 18:5–11)

10

The Force Is with You

"The Lord told me to drill to 2,600 feet. We did, and struck a new field that flowed 400 barrels of oil a day." That is Tom Brightman's description of how he began building an eighteen-million-dollar oil company in which he says God is the geologist. Brightman's wife, Mae, got the company name—Praise the Lord Drilling—from Proverbs 3:6: "In all your ways acknowledge him, and he will make straight your paths."

Pat Robertson, his voice and image known across the world through satellite TV transmission, says the day of miracles is not past. "We speak the word that arthritis be healed, that cysts be taken away." The founder of Christian Broadcasting Network (CBN), Robertson built a multimillion dollar television empire from public response to these concepts.

A slim woman stepped to the microphone at a church in St. Paul, Minnesota, and said in a soft voice: "I would like to share with you the way the Lord has led me in regard to my eating." Linda Waisanen proceeded to describe how she weighed more than 275 pounds before she turned to Jesus

Christ and asked him what to do. "Jesus led me to Overeaters Victorious," she said. "There he taught me the very real principles of discipline."

Norman Vincent Peale said in one of his syndicated newspaper columns, "When you place your full trust in God, when you practice God's presence, you become what I call a released person. You are released because you can defeat any weakness, solve any problem, and rise victorious over any defeat."

Each of these persons is drawing on another of Jesus' megatruths: *Entering God's kingdom releases a new power in your life and thought processes that transcends the normal cause and effect patterns of your environment.* Examples: "For truly I tell you, if you have faith the size of a mustard seed, you will say to this mountain, 'Move from here to there,' and it will move; and nothing will be impossible for you" (Matthew 17:20). "Whatever you ask for in prayer with faith, you will receive" (Matthew 21:22). In Luke 9:1–3, Jesus sends the seventy out with the power to heal the sick and tell them that the kingdom has come near to them. In Luke 10:17–20, he says that the seventy will have power over snakes and evil spirits. In Mark 16:17–18, he predicts that the eleven remaining disciples will have power to help the sick recover and to cast out demons, and will not be hurt by poisonous snakes. In Matthew 10:19–20, he tells the disciples that the words they need to say will be given to them in their hour of need (the same idea is expressed in Mark 13:11 and Luke 12:11–12; 21:13–15).

MEGATRUTH TEN

Entering God's kingdom releases a new power in your life and thought processes that transcends the normal cause and effect patterns of your environment.

Contemporary Americans of all ages have a deep yearning to believe this truth. The basic message of the movie "Star Wars" is that we can get in touch with and depend on the spiritual force of the universe. The amazing public acceptance of this old idea tells us that our rational, scientific minds have not outdistanced the deep longing of the human spirit for "something beyond." In another movie, "Damnation Alley," the boy says to the major, "Nothing good ever happens all by itself. You gotta' make it." The American public may, in times of despair, be tempted to think this is true. But we are not buying it at the box office. We are sticking with Jesus. Perhaps Augustine was right when he said in the fourth century that the human spirit is restless until it finds its rest in that Force. The scientific community cannot quite prove the presence of this Force. A month seldom passes, however, when it fails to produce additional bits and pieces of evidence that point toward powers which lie beyond the fringe of rationally understood cause and effect. Keith Harary, an experimental psychologist who worked at Duke University for many years, reported in *U.S. News and World Report* on an experiment in "remote viewing." He and a companion went to a site on the coast of Australia that they had picked from among thirty random possibilities. The spot held a little gazebo in a grass-filled park with a sidewalk leading up to it. The ocean could be seen in the background. Thirty miles away, a newspaper reporter—closeted in Harary's laboratory with no knowledge whatever of where Harary had gone—described an isolated building with grass around it and the ocean behind it, adding that there was a "path going up to the thing."

In another experiment, several subjects were able to predict the future. They were told that in fifteen minutes a person in another room would be given an object. A random-number selecting machine then picked a number, which designated the object the person was later to hold in his or her hand. An unbiased judge then compared what this "psychic viewer" described with what was actually held fifteen minutes later. Harary says, "How does it happen? We don't know, but it suggests that our understanding of space and time relationships is incomplete."

Medical science now recognizes that forces beyond

rationality can somehow interface with our physiological systems to keep us healthy. The human brain is a complex apothecary that produces thirty-four basic chemicals. Used in a variety of combinations, these chemicals can be mixed to produce homeostasis, a condition of chemical balance. The endorphins, for example, combat pain. Gamma globulin fortifies the immune system. Interferons combat infections, and evidence increasingly indicates they are important in fighting cancer. The brain can draw on these thirty-four secretions in an endless set of combinations, arming the human system with a protective response system of infinite response capacity. That is why some of the most successful treatments for fatal illnesses begin with the mind. If the brain adopts a certain attitude climate—through prayer, meditation, or other means—forces can come into play that make what had previously been impossible, possible.

The Christian faith has for twenty centuries produced substantiating evidences for Jesus' megatruth. Chaplain of the Senate Lloyd Ogilvie tells the story of George Mueller of Bristol, England. During a sixty-year ministry, Mueller raised more than 10,000 orphans during a period in history when this was a great social problem. One morning he was faced with the tragedy of running out of food for 2,000 youngsters. As they lined up at the long tables with their tin plates, he said, "Children, let's pray. Dear God, thank you for the food that you are about to bring." As the children looked down at their empty plates, a knock came at the door. It was a local baker. He said he had awakened at 2:00 a.m. with a distinct feeling that he should bake bread for the orphanage. So, here he was with the bread. After Mueller had distributed the bread, another knock came at the door. It was the milkman. His milk wagon had broken down in front of the orphanage. The only way he could get his wagon back for repair was to empty it. He wondered if Mr. Mueller could take the milk off his hands.

Across the centuries, evidence for this megatruth's validity has been added by persons of every theological persuasion. Many saints of the Roman Catholic Church engaged in miraculous healings and happenings (which were scrutinized by a panel of judges before they were granted sainthood). The Church of Christ, Scientist, founded in Boston in 1879 by Mary Baker Eddy, attempted to reinstate primitive Christianity and its lost element of healing. Although Mrs. Eddy died of cancer, records of that denomination contain many accounts which illustrate that Jesus was accurate in saying there is a Force beyond human force and reason. In more recent times, Oral Roberts of Tulsa, Oklahoma, has built a huge ministry and a university through emphasizing this teaching of Jesus. The contemporary charismatic movement is rife with examples of this megatruth. People helped by evangelist/healers of many kinds furnish evidence (which physicians say have no scientific explanation) of this teaching's validity.

Unfortunately, the evidence for this megatruth is not always consistent. This creates mental roadblocks for those who want to accept this teaching and credibility problems for those who wish to proclaim it. A couple interviewed on the Phil Donahue Show (December 24, 1979) reported that their sixteen-month-old son had died of meningitis after a period of more than two weeks in which Christian Science practitioners were praying for him. Their horror story (they are now very antagonistic toward their former faith) describes the progressive deterioration of the infant as the disease finally reached his brain and brought severe convulsions and partial paralysis. When the baby was gnashing his teeth, the practitioner said to the frightened parents, "Why don't you make a positive evaluation of the evidence? Maybe he isn't gnashing his teeth; maybe he is gritting his teeth because he is planning with anticipation some great achievement." The distraught mother said she had read in a Christian Science magazine the same month her son died: "Medicine is only a detour on the road to salvation."

This painful story illustrates an important principle: When this megatruth is carried to extremes (applied equally to every life circumstance), it becomes a form of religious insanity and countermands other equally important Christian teachings—love and concern for the needs of other persons and the use of common sense. "...for God did not give us a spirit of cowardice, but rather a spirit of power and of love and of self-discipline" (2 Timothy 1:7).

Inconsistent results in our contemporary experiences regarding this megatruth match the inconsistencies found in the New Testament record. On one hand, numerous examples of paranormal experiences and miracles are reported. On the other hand, the power to transcend the usual cause and effect relationships of physics and physiology is often withheld (even at times when it would seem to have advanced God's work). Some Christians needed healing but did not receive it (Epaphroditus in Philippians 2:26–27; Paul in 2 Corinthians 12:7; Timothy in 1 Timothy 5:23; and Trophimus in 2 Timothy 4:20). In three other instances, Aeneas, Eutychus, and Dorcas received the miraculous help they needed (Acts 9:34, 40; 20:7–12).

The apostle Paul said, "If God is for us, who is against us?" (Romans 8:31). "I can do all things through him who strengthens me" (Philippians 4:13). Paul and the other apostles frequently experienced this Power working through them (Acts 16:10; 20:9–12; 28:3–6, 8). Yet, Paul himself was not healed of the physical ailment that often prevented him from doing the work God had assigned him (2 Corinthians 12:7).

In spite of the biblical and experiential inconsistencies regarding this Force, Jesus clearly taught its availability. He says each of us has the potential to enter a different "level of consciousness" than the one we ordinarily utilize in daily life. Tapping into that puts us in touch with extraordinary powers of creativity, powers of insight, and powers of healing that we do not usually experience.

How do we enter this kingdom? By faith—by believing that it exists—by believing that God is real and can give us through this medium what we cannot achieve for ourselves through any other kind of thinking or action. When that happens, we move immovable mountains, dream and do impossible dreams, and move forward with courage that we never had.

God will not send you out to fell trees with a penknife. If he gives you a task you cannot do, he will give you a strength you do not have.

Discovery Questions for Group Discussion

1. Read John 14:12–14. Some scholars think the "greater works than these" of which Jesus speaks means his disciples will have the power to help people find a redemptive relationship with God. What do you think he means? Name some persons you know through whom God's power seems to work to do the impossible.

2. Read Matthew 17:19–21 and Matthew 21:21–22 (also found in Mark 9:23; 11:22; and Luke 17:5–6). Name some persons whose faith seems to have allowed God's power to help them do the impossible described here. Do they have personality qualities that seem to make them different from other people? If so, describe these qualities.

3. Read Mark 16:15–18. A few modern disciples seem to have the power described here. Some denominations teach that Christians no longer have this power. What do you think? Why?

4. Read John 16:23–24. Have you had experiences in which the truth of this text occurred in your life? Describe.

5. Read Luke 10:17–24 (also found in Matthew 11:25–27). Some denominations have based worship rituals and belief systems on this teaching. Do you feel positive or negative about that interpretation of this text? Why?

6. Read Acts 1:3–8. List the ways in which you have either observed or experienced the "power of the Holy Spirit" described in this text.

7. Do you think contemporary churches tend to neglect this megatruth? Illustrate.

8. Do you think some contemporary churches carry this megatruth to extremes? Illustrate.

9. What recommendations would you make to leaders of your local church regarding this megatruth?

Additional Examples

Jesus says we do not live by bread alone. (Matthew 4:4 and Luke 4:4).

Jesus tells those who labor and are heavy laden to come to him because his yoke is easy. (Matthew 11:28–30)

Jesus heals a leper. (Matthew 8:1–4; Mark 1:40–44; and Luke 5:12–14)

Jesus heals a centurion's servant. (Matthew 8:5–10, 13 and Luke 7:1–10)

Jesus calms the waves. (Matthew 8:23–27; Mark 4:35–41; and Luke 8:22–25)

Jesus casts demons into a herd of swine. (Matthew 8:28–34)

Jesus casts many demons out of a man living in tombs. (Mark 5:1–20 and Luke 8:22–39)

Jesus heals and forgives the paralytic. (Matthew 9:1–8; Mark 2:1–12; and Luke 5:17–26)

Jesus heals Jairus' daughter. (Matthew 9:18–19, 23–26; Mark 5:21–24, 35–43; and Luke 8:40–42, 49–56)

Jesus heals a woman with a hemorrhage. (Matthew 9:20–22; Mark 5:24–34; and Luke 8:42–48)

Jesus heals two blind men. (Matthew 9:27–31)

Jesus says that in his ministry the blind see, the lame walk, and the poor have good news preached to them. (Matthew 11:4–5 and Luke 7:22)

Jesus says he casts out demons by the power of God. (Matthew 12:24–29; Mark 3:22–27; and Luke 11:15–22)

Jesus feeds the multitudes. (Matthew 14:13–27; 15:32–39; Mark 6:30–44; 8:1–10; Luke 9:10–17; and John 6:1–14)

Jesus walks on the water. (Matthew 14:22–21; Mark 6:45–52; and John 6:16–21)

Jesus heals the daughter of a Canaanite woman. (Matthew 15:28 and Mark 7:29–30)

Jesus heals an epileptic. (Matthew 17:14–18; Mark 9:14–22, 25–27; and Luke 9:37–43)

Jesus directs Peter to take a coin for taxes from the mouth of a fish. (Matthew 17:24–27)

Jesus heals the blind. (Matthew 20:29–34; Mark 10:46–52; and Luke 18:35–43)

Without previous arrangements, an ass is provided for Jesus to ride. (Matthew 21:1–3; Mark 11:1–3; and Luke 19:28–31)

A place is provided for Jesus to celebrate the Passover meal. (Matthew 26:17–19; Mark 14:12–16; and Luke 22:7–13)

Jesus heals a man at Capernaum who has an unclean spirit. (Mark 1:21–28 and Luke 4:31–37)

Jesus heals a deaf man. (Mark 7:31–37)

Jesus heals a blind man. (Mark 8:22–26)

Jesus brings a dead man back to life at the city of Nain. (Luke 7:11–17)

Jesus heals a woman ill for eighteen years. (Luke 13:10–17)

Jesus heals ten lepers. (Luke 17:11–19)

Jesus meets Nathanael and reveals that he has the power to know all about him prior to their meeting. (John 1:47–50)

Jesus turns water into wine. (John 2:1–11)

Jesus heals the son of an official at Capernaum. (John 4:46–54)

Jesus heals a paralyzed man by the pool who has been ill for thirty-eight years. (John 5:1–18)

Jesus heals a man blind from birth. (John 9:1–7)

Jesus raises Lazarus from the dead. (John 11:43–44)

Jesus implies that God will be glorified (honored) through the power illustrated in Jesus' living beyond death. (John 13:31–33; 14:28–31)

Jesus says the disciples have the power to see what is and is not a part of God's kingdom. He uses a rabbinic term that means "forbid and permit," referring to action about which questions will arise in the church. (Matthew 18:15–19; 16:19; and John 20:22–23)

Jesus says those who live by his words will receive from God whatever they ask. (John 15:7)

Jesus says whatever the disciples ask in his name will be given to them. (John 15:16)

Speaking of his "thorn in the flesh," Paul says Jesus tells him that his power is greater when it appears in the midst of weakness. (2 Corinthians 12:7–9)

11

Joy Is a Personality Detergent

The waitress could not get a smile out of her customer. All through dinner, the woman seemed dour and dejected. The food wasn't that bad, and the service was excellent. As the lady paid her bill on the way out, the waitress tried one last time. "Have a nice day!" she said cheerily. The woman snapped back with, "I'm sorry, but I have made other plans."

The University of Houston has produced more winning golfers than anyplace else in the world. Dave Williams, head golf coach, was asked in a radio interview what he thought was the most important thing in golf. He replied, "The most important thing about golf is in your *head*. It is so easy to get upset, angry, mentally off-center."

The famous pulpit giant of a previous generation Charles Spurgeon was addressing a group of divinity students. "When you talk to people about heaven," he said, "let your face light up with a heavenly glory. When you talk about hell, your everyday face will probably do."

These three snapshots from the passing parade of human personality point to a deep need met by another of Jesus' megatruths: *Entering God's kingdom enables you to live joyfully.* Examples: After Jesus gives his twelve disciples the analogy about the vine and the branches, he says, "I have said these things to you so that my joy may be in you, and that your joy may be complete" (John 15:11). In John 10:10, Jesus says, "I came that they may have life, and have it abundantly." In Matthew 9:14–17, he says that his disciples don't fast because they have the Christ with them. In John 16:22, he predicts that he will see the disciples again and that their hearts will rejoice.

Members of the contemporary charismatic movement have helped balance some of the theological deficiencies to which mainline denominations have been prone in recent decades. One of their most important contributions has been the recapturing of joy as a part of the Christian experience. They have put us back in touch with the big difference between *happiness* and *joy.*

MEGATRUTH ELEVEN

Entering God's kingdom enables you to live joyfully.

When people say they want to be *happy,* they usually mean they want to get their circumstances right. Examples: She has a happy marriage. He is happy in his work. She cannot be happy unless she makes straight A's. He will be happy if he wins first prize. The team will be deliriously happy if it wins the World Series.

Joy, on the other hand, is an attitude that does not depend on the soil of circumstances. It is an air plant that draws its nutrients from a different kingdom. New Testament Christians didn't have great circumstances, but they had great joy. Jesus told them that God loved them and nothing could separate them from that—not even death. That good news was an attitude detergent which kept them clean of despair, even in despairing circumstances. As the early church expanded across Asia Minor, the apostles thanked God that they were counted worthy to suffer for Christ's sake (Acts 5:41). When Paul and Barnabas aroused the anger of several respected, religious women and some of the leading citizens in Antioch of Pisidia, they were persecuted and expelled from the district. Undaunted, the two pioneer preachers shook the dust off their feet in protest and moved on to Iconium. The next verse says, "And the disciples were filled with joy and with the Holy Spirit" (Acts 13:52). A few years later, Paul wrote from a prison cell where he was awaiting trial, "Rejoice in the Lord always; again I will say, Rejoice" (Philippians 4:4). These texts illustrate why someone said, "In the New Testament, joyful music is so persistent that reading it is like entering a bird sanctuary on a spring morning." This pervasive joy spilled over into the first-century church and beyond: Barnabas called Christians "children of joy." Clement of Alexandria, writing in the mid-second century says, "Praising we plow, singing we sail." Tertullian, the lawyer, writes about A.D. 150, "The Church is the one thing in the world that always rejoices." In the sixteenth century, Martin Luther was amazed that St. Agatha, lying in prison, "was as happy as if she were at a dance." Those who enter Jesus' kingdom, because they trust God, can be joyful in desperate circumstances. They have their confidence in the right place, and it sustains them.

That is why Leslie Weatherhead, the great English pastor, said, "The opposite of joy is not sorrow. It is unbelief." That is why Elton Trueblood wrote in *The Humor of Christ*, "It is not really surprising, therefore, that the Christian should laugh and sing; after all he has a great deal to laugh about. He understands, with George Fox, that, though there is an ocean of darkness and death, there is also an ocean of light and love which flows over the ocean of darkness."[+]

We look for joy in vain if we seek it in circumstances, geographical surroundings, and human relationships. That kind of search always fails because it does not bring us to God. "Strive for the kingdom of God and his righteousness," Jesus said, "and all these things will be given to you as well" (Matthew 6:33). We must first come to God, if we intend to come to joy. In that relationship, and that alone, are we lifted

---

[+](New York: Harper & Row, 1964.)

to the stable jet stream high above the changing winds of surface circumstances.

Too many Christians hear the *words* of scripture but not the *music*. Faith is the words. Joy is the music.

Discovery Questions for Group Discussion

1. Read Luke 5:33–39 (also found in Matthew 9:14–17 and Mark 2:18–22). Do you think some denominations, like the Pharisees described here, have communicated the idea that being a disciple is a somber and dreary experience? Illustrate.

2. Read John 17:13. Describe Christians you know who exhibit the genuine sense of joy expressed in this text. List factors that you feel cause such persons to have this joy that eludes other Christians.

3. Read John 16:16–24. Jesus predicts that the day is coming when no one can take their joy from them. Share the ideas or methods you have personally found most helpful in keeping joy a central part of your life.

4. Do you think contemporary churches tend to neglect this megatruth? Illustrate.

5. Do you think some contemporary churches carry this megatruth to extremes? Illustrate.

6. What advice would you like to give leaders of your local church regarding this megatruth?

12

God's Good Night

In one of history's most decisive battles, Wellington was locked in combat with the infamous Napoleon at Waterloo. News of the final result could not come back to London by radio or telegraph. Neither had been invented yet. All England waited breathlessly as the word crossed the channel by sailboat and overland by a relay of semaphore signals.

From the top of Winchester Cathedral in southern England, a semaphore began to spell out the message letter by letter: "Wellington defeated." The next link in the relay of semaphores caught this message just as dense fog settled in and obliterated the flashing light. Those two words shrouded Londoners with a gloom and despair thicker than the fog. All was lost.

After the mist lifted, the Winchester Cathedral signaler sent his message again, just to be sure it got through: "Wellington defeated...the enemy." What a difference these two extra words made in London. Gloom became gladness. The mad Frenchman was overcome. England was safe. The future was secure.

Similar reversals appear between Saturday and Sunday of Easter week. On Saturday, the message was bleak: "Jesus defeated. The miracle worker is dead and buried. A big boulder seals his body in a rock tomb. It is all over." But Sunday sunrise brought new news: "He is risen. What he taught is true. Death is not the final word."

Archaeologists excavating ancient Roman cemeteries found seven letters on nearly all the grave stones: "NF F NS NC." Four brief sentences were so familiar to all Romans that the first letters of the words were sufficient to bring them to mind: "Non fui. Fui. Non sum. Non cure." They translate, "I was not. I was. I am not. I do not care." The ancient world lived under this white flag of surrender to the finality of death.

Against this assumption, the Galilean carpenter flung another of his megatruths: *If you enter God's kingdom, you will continue to live in that consciousness beyond the time of physical death.* Examples: "My sheep hear my voice. I know them, and they follow me. I give them eternal life, and they will never perish. No one will snatch them out of my hand" (John 10:27). "For God so loved the world that he gave his only Son, so that everyone who believes in him may not perish but may have eternal life"

MEGATRUTH TWELVE

If you enter God's kingdom, you will continue to live in that consciousness beyond the time of physical death.

(John 3:16). Similar statements appear in Matthew 25:46; John 3:15; 4:14; 5:24; 6:27, 40, 47, 54; 10:28; 12:25; and 17:2–3. Just as "kingdom of God" and "kingdom of heaven" are synonymous terms in all Jesus' teachings, he uses "enter the kingdom" and "inherit eternal life" to mean the same thing. Clear examples of this usage appear in Mark 10:24–30; Matthew 19:23–29; and Luke 18:24–30.

This megatruth is vastly *different* from the others and from the teachings of other world religions. Much more than propositional and philosophical, it is experiential and observational. Jesus backed it up by transcending his own death. Socrates was wise, but he didn't survive the hemlock.

Mohammed amassed a great following, but his memorial is a tomb, not an empty tomb. Confucius voiced brilliant observations on the human condition, but his students cannot report that he is still alive.

A Quaker standing on the seashore in the days of the great double-masted schooners watched a ship spread her white sails in the morning breeze. Moving out into the blue ocean, the beautiful vision gradually diminished to a tiny white feather on the horizon. As she slipped out of view, someone standing beside him, said, "There, she's gone!" Had she actually changed sizes and disappeared? No! This distortion comes from our limited perspective. From where we stand, it seems sensible to say of someone who dies, "There! She's gone!" According to Jesus, this is not the whole picture. He says there is no diminishing of life at the horizon of death. Using his viewpoint, we could just as easily say, "There! There she comes!"

Prior to the time of Christ, mourners buried their deceased family members facing the west—toward sunset and the darkness of night. After the resurrection, burial customs reversed. Lost loved ones now faced east. The night of death became the prelude to a new tomorrow. In Paul's listing of leaders in the early church, he ranks apostles first and healers fifth (1 Corinthians 12:28). Why? Because Christians saw the human spirit as permanent and the human body as temporary. American Christians in recent decades have tended in the opposite direction, concentrating more on the now and here. But this contemporary anomaly is much more determined by our own generation's view of reality than by New Testament teachings. Jesus taught the importance of *both*: Life is important, but there is more to life than life.

The Christian sects that rise out of deprived environments and harsh periods of history speak of this megatruth frequently. John's book of Revelation in the New Testament furnishes a good example. During the decade of intense Christian persecution when it was written, many were dying daily for their beliefs. No wonder they read and preserved what has today become a mysterious and difficult-to-comprehend book. It offered them hope for the future in a present that held nothing but despair. Slaves in the early American South shared this experience of oppression with John's audience. Their strong hope about the afterlife was woven into the great Negro spirituals, which still provide a theological base for many black denominations.

An African-American pastor conducting a funeral service turned to the casket and began addressing the deceased person. In a tasteful way, the preacher told him all the beautiful things people wished they had told him while he was alive. Completing the sermon, he said, "That's it, Clarence. That's it. Got nothing more to say. When you got nothing more to say, Clarence, there is only one thing to say." Reaching up, he grabbed the casket lid and slammed it down. "Good night, Clarence."

Turning to the congregation, he added, "And I know the Lord is going to give Clarence a good morning." With those words, the choir began to sing, "On that great gettin' up morning, we shall rise, we shall rise." Not a bad translation of Jesus' megatruth. Death is the *good* night that prepares us for God's good morning.

Discovery Questions for Group Discussion

1. Read John 3:9–21. Do you think this megatruth is taught more or less in our denomination than it was twenty years ago? Do you like or dislike this trend? Why?

2. Read John 6:32–40. Jesus appears to say that giving eternal life is the main purpose of his life. What danger does a contemporary church face if it focuses on this teaching to the exclusion of others?

3. Read John 8:51. What danger does a contemporary church face if it totally disregards the megatruth expressed in the text above?

4. Read John 14:1–4. This text is frequently read at funeral services. Have you found this to be of comfort in such situations? Are there times when it produces more discomfort than comfort for the family? If so, how do you think pastors should handle that type of funeral?

5. Read John 20:19–20. Jesus illustrates the truth about life after death by appearing alive to the disciples. Most people feel that without the resurrection the Christian faith would have no value. Do you agree or disagree? Why?

6. Have you experienced times in your life when this teaching was extremely helpful? Illustrate.

7. As you think of the various sociological strata of our contemporary society and world, do you see reasons why this teaching would be more appropriate for some persons than others? Illustrate.

8. What recommendations would you like to give the shapers of theological thinking and teaching in your denomination regarding this megatruth?

Additional Examples

Jesus tells the disciples that his living beyond death was predicted by Old Testament prophets. (Luke 24:45–46)

Jesus says those who have done good will have eternal life. (John 5:29)

Jesus says those who hate their life in this world will find eternal life. (John 12:25, 32)

Jesus tells the Jews that those who believe in him will have eternal life. (John 5:21, 24)

Jesus tells the Samaritan woman at the well that those who believe in him will have eternal life. (John 4:7–15)

Jesus says he gives his sheep eternal life. (John 10:27–28)

At the time he raises Lazarus from the dead, Jesus says those who believe in him will never die. (John 11:25–27)

Jesus says God commands eternal life for those who follow him. (John 12:50)

Jesus says he will live beyond three days of death. (John 2:18–22)

Jesus commits his spirit to God as he dies. (Luke 23:46 and John 19:30)

Jesus lives beyond death and meets the women at the tomb. (Matthew 28:9–10 and John 20:14–18)

Jesus lives beyond death and talks with the disciples on the road to Emmaus. (Luke 24:13–32)

Jesus appears to the disciples gathered in Jerusalem. (Luke 24:33–44)

Jesus proves himself alive by appearing to Thomas eight days after his meeting with the disciples behind locked doors. (John 20:26–29)

Jesus lives beyond death and meets the disciples on the seashore. (John 21:4–22)

Jesus appears alive to the disciples and promises the Holy Spirit. (Acts 1:3–8)

Jesus appears alive to Paul and Ananias and instructs Paul to serve him as a witness. (Acts 9:1–19; 22:6–21; 23:11)

Jesus appears to Paul in Corinth. (Acts 9:5–11)

13

What the World Needs Now

One evening in the late 1880s, Henry Drummond was visiting friends at their home in England. A group had gathered for informal conversation. When someone asked Drummond to name his favorite passage of scripture, he took a New Testament from his pocket and read from the thirteenth chapter of First Corinthians.

Among the listeners was Dwight L. Moody, the great American evangelist. He was so impressed by Drummond's remarks that he invited him to come to his school in Chicago and deliver them as an address. Drummond did, and it was so well received that the school had it read every year. Published in a small booklet entitled "The Greatest Thing in the World," it is still available today. The title seems presumptuous, but it came directly out of the passage Drummond had read: "And now faith, hope, and love abide, these three; and the greatest of these is love" (1 Corinthians 13:13).

When William James' son, Billy, came to visit his uncle in 1902, Henry James told him: "Three things in human life are important. The first is to be kind. The second is to be kind. And the third is to be kind." When the great saint-philosopher Baron Fredrich von Hugel lay dying, his niece bent over him to hear what his moving lips were saying. Putting her ear close to his mouth, she heard his last words: "Caring is everything; nothing else matters." Though this is not the *only* thing in human life that matters, it surely appears near the top of everyone's quality-of-life list. A line from a song says, "What the world needs now is love, sweet love." It always has and always will. As Mother Teresa put it, "Being unwanted is the worst disease any human being can experience. Unless there are willing hands to serve and a loving heart to care, it is uncurable." Each of us needs a relationship with people who think well of us and know how to express it. Far greater than the power of the pen, the sword, or science is the power of love to alter individual existence for the better.

But this four-letter religious word does more than meet our *personal* need. It is the driving motive behind all institutional and governmental progress. Over the centuries, it has inspired everything from the establishment of hospitals and schools to prison reform and the abolition of slavery. When a county zoning board in Mt. Vernon, Virginia, barred the use of churches as shelters for the homeless because it was not a "religious activity," they aroused the ire of the secular as well as the religious citizens.

MEGATRUTH THIRTEEN

Entering God's kingdom gives you increased love and concern for other people.

Rev. Vin A. Harwell of the Mt. Vernon Presbyterian Church knew he could count on public as well as congregational affirmation when he told the zoning board, "Sheltering the homeless is as much a part of what we do as our Sunday worship."

It is not, therefore, surprising to find an emphasis on this four-letter word among Jesus' megatruths: *Entering God's kingdom gives you increased love and concern for other people.* Examples: "You shall love your neighbor as yourself" (Matthew 22:39). In Luke 10:25–37, Jesus used the parable of the good Samaritan to connect loving God with the qualities of neighborliness and mercy, vividly asserting that loving God always involves an increased awareness of and concern for the needs of others. In Luke 14:12–14, he urges us to invite the poor to our banquets.

Prominent among religious groups that lean heavily on this megatruth are The Religious Society of Friends in the U.S., often called Quakers. This teaching buttresses their central doctrine of social, economic, interracial, and international justice. What some of the monastic orders of earlier centuries retreated to monasteries to do in the way of service, the "Friends" try to accomplish by advancing into political structures and areas of critical human need across the world. Though strongly nonviolent, their conviction against soldiering is accompanied by an equally strong willingness to face personal risk in administering relief to the victims of war. Chairperson Stephen Carey, addressing an annual meeting of the American Friends Service Committee, said, "Quakerism is not hung on the wall or put in a frame. Quakerism is daring. Quakerism is going out in the world to make a difference."

Another denomination based on this teaching started when William Booth of England left the Methodist New Connection Body in 1865 to organize his street work under the name of Christian Mission—which, in 1878, he changed to Salvation Army. This group eventually produced the most intelligent and widespread social welfare program in Christendom. It gives aid to the homeless, the sick, unemployed and unemployable (in India, the East Indies, and the Celebes thousands of lepers have been treated in their hospitals), unmarried mothers, criminals in prison and released from prison, children, and the aged.

Church World Service, the relief arm of the National Council of Churches, leans heavily on this megatruth when it mounts campaigns to feed the world's hungry. Much of the continuing support for this controversial ecumenical institution rests on public affirmation of benevolent work of this sort.

But despite the fact that this is one of Jesus' clearest and most publicly supported teachings, it is among the most difficult to practice—even for religious people. A sign on a convent in California summarizes the ever-present paradox of Christian life: "Absolutely No Trespassing. Violators Will Be Persecuted to the Full Extent of the Law! Signed: The Sisters of Mercy."

In a play entitled "John Brown's Body," Stephen Vincent Benet pictures the captain of a slave ship who is faithful in his prayers but sees nothing wrong with his traffic in human bodies. Tradition says that Sir John Bowring, while serving as British governor of Hong Kong, promoted the opium trade with China. Yet, Sir John also authored a Christian hymn sung by millions each week: "In the cross of Christ I glory; Towering o'er the wrecks of time." Those who have been deeply involved in church work see truth in the old proverb "To live above with the saints we love, oh, that will be glory. But to live below with the folks we know, ah, that's a different story."

Why is this? If we all agree on this megatruth, why do we have so much difficulty acting out our thoughts and verbalizations? Mostly because of our predisposition toward self-centeredness. The extreme form of this tendency from which we all suffer is illustrated in the story of a movie actress at a large reception. Engaged in conversation with a stranger, she chatted for thirty minutes about her glowing press releases, her triumphs as a starlet, and her glamorous family. Suddenly, she interrupted her monologue by saying, "Oh, dear, here I've been carrying on about me, and I've hardly given you a chance to talk. Tell me, what do you think about my last movie?"

This basic self-centeredness (which the Bible calls sin) causes us to emphasize love at the thinking level rather than the action level. The catchy commercial for a new wine showed one friend giving the other an empty wine box. "What can I do with an empty box?" responds the gift recipient. "It's the thought that counts," says the giver. Jesus discounts the validity of that quip in every statement and parable on this subject. The thought weighs very little on his scales. The kind of love he teaches always moves beyond thinking into acting. It is not just an emotion—it is a motion. Actions do always *begin* with thoughts, but thoughts alone never heal the hurt, bind up the wound, feed the hungry, clothe the naked, and say the kind word. A Buddhist teacher was close to Jesus' meaning of love when he said, "To know and not to do is not really yet to know." Someone said, "Love reduces friction to a fraction." But it is not the thought that does this; it is the action and the *reaction*.

Cherry Blossom Park is a beautiful spot in Portland, Oregon. In the spring, when the blossoms are in full strength, it is aflame with color. But these trees are in one sense quite deceptive. They blossom, but they never bear any fruit. That is why they are called Flowering Cherry Trees. Love that only thinks and talks is not love at all. It is a self-deception born of our inner drive toward self-centeredness.

How can we overcome this centripetal force which drives us to center in on self rather than center out on others? Jesus says the best remedy is to enter the new level of consciousness that he calls the kingdom of God.

One of the first marks of recovery for a mentally ill person is the ability to show concern and compassion for other people. Jesus says this is also one of the first marks of a person who begins to recover from living outside the new level of consciousness which he calls the kingdom of God.

Discovery Questions for Group Discussion

1. Read Matthew 22:36–40 (also found in Mark 12:31–34 and Luke 10:27–28). Jesus says that along with recognizing that God is here and loving him, those who enter the kingdom of God will love other people. Someone has described Christians as falling into three groups:

those who relate well to God but not to other people; those who relate well to other people but not to God; and those who do both. Have you known persons who fall into each of these categories? Describe each kind of person.

2. Read John 13:34–35. Do you think people in some contemporary congregations do better at fulfilling this text than others do? What factors do you think create these differences?

3. Read Luke 10:25–37. Jesus says that people of the kingdom do acts of love toward all other persons, regardless of their religious views or tradition. Yet, the last 2,000 years of religious wars and denominational controversy tell us this has not happened a great deal. Are there ways in which our denomination has violated this teaching? What do you think we should do to help improve this situation?

4. Read Matthew 5:42–48 and Matthew 7:12. Name some ways in which the U.S. government has practiced the truth of this text during the last fifty years. Are there ways in which you feel they have disregarded it?

5. In his numerous healings on the Jewish Sabbath (examined in chapters 3 and 10), Jesus shows that loving people is more important than religious rituals or traditions. Examples: Luke 13:10–17; 14:1–6; and John 5:1–18; 7:21–24. As denominations grow older, they have a tendency to begin acting like these religious officials and start giving more value to tradition than to loving people. Are there any ways in which you think that is true in our denomination?

6. Is it possible to emphasize this truth too much? Explain your opinion.

7. What advice would you like to give our local church leaders regarding this megatruth?

Additional Examples

Jesus says that the merciful are blessed. (Matthew 5:7) Jesus prays that the love by which God has loved him will be in the disciples. (John 17:26)

Jesus says the disciples are to love each other as he has loved them by giving them God's words and sacrificing his life for them. (John 15:9–10, 12–15, 17)

14

Is Good Judgment Bad Behavior?

New beginnings were everywhere. History had just given birth to a new nation. Pioneers pressed through the Cumberland Gap and down the Ohio River. Easterners were claiming land in the west—Illinois, Indiana, and Kentucky.

Alexander Campbell and Barton Stone found this soil fertile for innovation. Reacting against the intolerance they had left behind in European churches, they hoped for something better in America. They didn't find it there when they arrived. The colonists had already started replicating the religious antagonisms from which they had fled. But people were ready to hear a better word. They were tired of religious bickering.

Campbell and Stone were not short on words. "The blowing of denominational trumpets doesn't raise the dead and is very offensive to our neighbors," said Campbell. "In essentials, unity; in opinion, liberty; in all things, love." This new idea's day had come. Hundreds of thousands responded. The largest Christian movement born on American soil came into being: The Christian Church (Disciples of Christ) and its cousins, the Churches of Christ and the Independent Christian Churches.

Campbell, Stone, and the countless others who took up their banner during the next 190 years derived much of their conviction from another of Jesus' megatruths: *Entering God's kingdom makes you less judgmental about other people.* Examples: "Do not judge, so that you may not be judged" (Matthew 7:1). In Matthew 13:24–30, Jesus illustrates the principle of leaving judgment to God instead of trying to do it ourselves.

Few new denominations launch on this teaching, probably because most splinter groups are quite judgmental. They usually *begin* by strongly judging and criticizing the practices or neglects of their mother church. The "Disciples" and "Christian" Church congregations of the early nineteenth century were certainly critical of the denominational status quo. Yet, they nailed a tolerance plank into their theological platform: "We are not the only Christians, but Christians only," was one of their mottos. While trying to unite all Christians into one body, adherents were urged to avoid making

MEGATRUTH FOURTEEN

Entering God's kingdom makes you less judgmental about other people.

judgments about who would or would not achieve heaven. If people believed in Christ and were baptized, they were accepted as members.

The Unitarian Churches in England and America (considered a quasi-Christian movement by some) developed an even broader stance regarding those who held divergent beliefs. They tried to nonjudgmentally weave all religious threads into a single plaid blanket. In his famous Baltimore sermon of 1819, William Ellery Channing of Boston outlined the Unitarian view: "By his Church, our Savior does not mean a party bearing the name of a human leader, distinguished by a form or an opinion, and on the ground of this distinction, denying the name and character of Christians to all but themselves...."

The Baha'i religion, though not Christian by the standard definition of that term, uses this teaching of Jesus to promote its aims for the unity of all religions and the abandonment of all prejudices. Its leader, Baha'u'llah, said, "The religion of God is for the sake of love and union; make it not the cause of enmity and conflict."

The Federated Churches in the U.S., a largely rural and village phenomenon, are not really a sect or denomination but an assortment of individual congregations. Strongest in New England and the West, such churches usually arise where two or more small congregations representing different denominations unite for mutual conduct of their work while continuing their connections with their respective denominations. They cooperate without requiring conformity on doctrinal matters, and they deliberately restrain themselves from making religious judgments about each other. Most federated churches, however, arise from pragmatic shortfalls of funds and potential members. Few of them are formed because of the idealistic desire to follow biblical doctrines of Christian unity.

In more recent decades, many American churches have tried to make this megatruth more operable in their organizational lives. The United Church of Christ was formed in 1957 through the merger of the Congregational Christian Churches and the Evangelical and Reformed Church. In 1968, the Evangelical United Brethrens and the Methodists formed the United Methodist Church. During the early 1980s, northern and southern Presbyterian bodies, disunited in 1861 Civil War days, welded together into the Presbyterian Church (U.S.A.). Three Lutheran denominations recently voted to form a new Lutheran Church. For the first time since the Protestant Reformation in the early 1600s, a Roman Catholic pope, John Paul, participated in a Lutheran service. On December 11, 1983, he and a Lutheran pastor, Christoph Meyer, joined in reciting a prayer written by Luther for Christian unity, and the pope preached a sermon on the reconciliation of all Christians.

Do members of these denominations extend their nonjudgmental stance into personal life? That is a different question altogether. Withholding judgment when someone commits a personal offense against you is far more difficult than refraining from criticisms regarding church doctrine. Jesus seems to have *both* categories in mind. Judgment is one of the few instances in which we should give more generously to ourselves than to our friends. Judgment, like love, multiplies when you give it away. But it isn't nearly as much fun to receive back.

Discovery Questions for Group Discussion

1. Read Matthew 7:1–5 (also found in Luke 6:37–38, 41–42). Do you think Jesus is talking about every type of judgment? Does his statement apply to our court system? Does it apply to our grading system in schools? To precisely what areas of life do you think this megatruth does apply?

2. Read John 8:3–11. Jesus says that since all have sinned, no one should judge the woman caught in adultery. Do you think this means we are to make no judgments whatever about the behavior of other persons? How, for example, should a church leader apply this principle to a young adult Sunday school class in which wife-swapping began to occur? Do you think Jesus means we are not to judge, or do you think he means we are not to physically or emotionally injure other people with our judgments?

3. Read Matthew 13:24–30 and Matthew 13:36–39. Jesus says that we should leave judgment to God. How do you think this injunction applies to our judgments about people in other denominations? To people with whom we disagree on church policy? What are some practical ways in which churches can help their members become less judgmental?

4. Think of the most nonjudgmental person you have ever known. Did his/her attitude seem to have a positive effect on people around him/her? Illustrate.

5. Do you think contemporary churches practice this megatruth more now than four decades ago? Illustrate your opinion.

6. Do you think it is possible for a church to carry this megatruth to extremes? Illustrate your opinion.

7. What recommendations do you have for leaders of your local church regarding this megatruth?

15

Carrying Out the Trash

On May 13, 1981, Mehmet Ali Agca shot Pope John Paul II. On January 9, 1984, *TIME* magazine's cover pictured the pope with his left arm around the assassin's shoulder and his right hand clasping Agca's in a firm handshake.

In a New Hampshire town whose economy was devastated by the early 1980s recession, a variety store owner "wrote off" almost $10,000 in debts owed by 1,200 customers. "Start fresh with us," the store's newspaper ad said.

The movie *Gandhi* contains a scene from the time of violent civil strife in India between Hindus and Muslims. A brokenhearted Hindu father comes to Gandhi, saying that his only son has been killed by Muslim rioters. He asks Gandhi what he can do to compensate for this injustice. "You must find a Muslim boy who has no father," Gandhi says, "and bring him up as a Muslim!"

Edwin Stanton, a Democrat, was highly critical of Abraham Lincoln. Calling him a "low, cunning clown" and "the original gorilla," Stanton said that zoologists were foolish to look in Africa for what they could so easily have found in Springfield, Illinois. Everyone was amazed when Lincoln appointed Stanton Secretary of War. When asked why,

Lincoln replied that he was the best man for the job. Near the end of the Civil War, Lincoln was telling a group of White House visitors about his plans to treat the South leniently after the war. A guest objected with, "But Mr. President, I would think you would want to destroy your enemies." Lincoln replied with, "Don't I destroy my enemies when I make them my friends?"

These diverse stories have a common thread. The attitude of each leading character is based on another of Jesus' megatruths: *Entering God's kingdom gives you a more forgiving spirit.* Examples: "Then Peter came and said to him, 'Lord, if another member of the church sins against me, how often should I forgive? As many as seven times?' Jesus said to him, 'Not seven times, but, I tell you, seventy-seven times'" (Matthew 18:21–22). In Matthew 18:23–35, Jesus illustrates with the parable about an unforgiving debtor the need for showing mercy on those who wrong us. In Matthew 5:21–26, he warns against anger. In Luke 6:27–28, he speaks of the need to turn the other cheek. When

MEGATRUTH FIFTEEN

Entering God's kingdom gives you a more forgiving spirit.

Jesus meets his friends on the seashore in John 21:1–20— friends who have failed him at his moment of greatest need— we hear no reproaches. Jesus does not say, "Peter, you deserted me there in the courtyard while I was on trial for my life." Instead, we hear words like, "Look out there ahead, Peter. My sheep need your help. You can do it. Go feed them." We do not hear Jesus saying to James and John, "You really let me down there in the Garden of Gethsemane. I was struggling to find the courage to face death, and you took a nap." Instead, we hear words like, "Go into all the world and represent me. I will be with you all the way, even to the end of the world."

As with its similar but slightly different partner (Megatruth Number Fourteen regarding judgmental attitudes in the previous chapter) few sects are born out of a focus on this teaching of Jesus. Human beings do not often or easily band together for such a passive purpose as forgiving their enemies. This teaching is, however, a strong thread in many nonresistance sects that spring up during times of war. When the military draft of the American Civil War reached into the ranks of the River Brethren Church, a group of them split off in 1862 to adopt the name Brethren in Christ. Nonresistance was not their only tenet, but it became the primary theology behind their forming of a new denomination. More recently, several contemporary denominations based their merger decisions, at least in part, on this determination to live out a forgiving attitude. The recent union of two Presbyterian bodies separated since the American Civil War is one example; that of two Lutheran bodies separated by theological viewpoints is another.

We should not be surprised to find so few *totally new* denominations springing to life on a forgiveness foundation. What other teaching of Jesus runs so utterly contrary to our natural reflexes? F. Scott Fitzgerald was an American author whose novels sold well in the 1920s and 1930s. Perhaps the most famous of these was *The Great Gatsby*. When Fitzgerald died, the outline of a new book was found on his desk. The plot involved a family that had been fragmented over the years by disagreements and wrangling. It began with this family seated in a lawyer's office to hear the reading of a wealthy aunt's will. The lawyer informed the family that each was to receive an enormous fortune—on one condition, that they learn to live together in the same house. Fitzgerald's book likely would have sold well. It accurately depicts the lives of so many people—and the concurrent wish that things could be better in relationships gone sour.

Splashed across the center of the *TIME* magazine cover showing the pope forgiving his enemy were these words in large letters: "Why forgive?" We all ask this question at moments of deep injustice. Why should we forgive, especially if the person has not asked for our forgiveness? The question has at least three good answers.

First of all, not forgiving damages us psychologically. A

pygmy rattlesnake at the Grant Park Zoo in Atlanta, Georgia, died after accidentally biting itself on the lip while trying to swallow a meal. A zoo spokesman explained the incident by saying that some snakes are susceptible to their own venom. An unforgiving heart is like rattlesnake venom and certain kinds of acid. It can damage the container in which it is stored as much as the object on which it is poured.

George C. Scott, playing the role of oil field hand Noble Mason in the movie *Oklahoma Crude,* says to the heroine's father, "You can't ever get back at anybody. Don't you know that?" Many persons who are far better educated and acculturated than Noble Mason do not know that. They keep on hurting themselves while trying to get even with other people. As someone else has said, "It is far better to forgive and forget than to resent and remember." Or, as a Catholic psychiatrist remarked to John Claypool, "Forgiveness is the only creative solution to human imperfection."

Forgiveness unhooks the forgiver from the continual pain of not forgiving. It saves us the energy-consuming task of carrying a grudge. It unties us from a painful and continual reliving of past memories involving the bad things the person has said and done to us. Someone said that people who forget history are doomed to repeat it. But it is equally true that those who cannot forget and forgive past wrongs in their histories are doomed to mentally relive them.

Second, not forgiving damages our ability to experience life's deepest meanings. In Victor Hugo's novel *Les Miserables,* Jean Valjean has become a criminal through the suffering of gross inhumanities. After serving a prison term, he emerges with the determination to do by others as he has been done by, only more so. After stealing the candlesticks of a bishop who has befriended him, he is arrested. In his confrontation with the bishop and the police, the bishop unexpectedly lies. He says he gave him the candlesticks. After the authorities leave the two men alone, Jean wants to know why the bishop saved him. The words with which the bishop replies change the criminal's life: "Remember, Jean, life is to give, not to take." The first half of the word "forgive" means "to go ahead of." People who experience life's deepest meanings know that life is to give, not to take. So, they give first.

Third, not forgiving damages us spiritually. It opens a relational gap between us and the God whose nature it is to forgive. One of the first places we detect this break is in our prayer life. That is why Jesus warns us in Mark 11:25–26 that if we want the peace that comes with true prayer and worship, we must first go and forgive the person who has wronged us—not just seek forgiveness from those we have wronged but forgive those who have wronged us.

But how can we ever find the power to reverse our naturally resentful human instincts? We can't! Not by ourselves. That is precisely Jesus' point. Only to those who enter the kingdom level of consciousness does this power come.

A four-year-old had not clearly understood the prayer he heard so frequently in church. His mother was amazed one day when she overheard him praying: "And forgive us our trashbaskets as we forgive those who put trash in our baskets."

But, then, maybe he was right.

Discovery Questions for Group Discussion

1. Read Matthew 5:38–41 (also found in Luke 6:27–29). Jesus says that people who enter the kingdom are willing to let those who wrong them have the opportunity to do that wrong again. Can you give historical illustrations from this century in which the U.S. government seems to have practiced this principle? Have you had personal experiences in which you tried to use this principle? How did it work out?

2. Read Matthew 18:21–22 (also found in Luke 17:3–4). Jesus suggests that God-conscious people are able to forgive an infinite number of times. Describe the most forgiving person you ever knew. Did his/her forgiving spirit appear to call for great financial or emotional sacrifices?

3. Read Matthew 6:12 (also found in Luke 11:4) and Matthew 6:14–15 (also found in Mark 11:25–26). In this text from the Lord's Prayer and many others in the New Testament, Jesus links the willingness to forgive with God's willingness to forgive us and our ability to communicate with him in prayer. Do you think that is true in all cases of nonforgiveness? Do you remember any personal incidents in which you experienced the truth of this principle in your own life?

4. Read Luke 23:34. Jesus forgave those who had driven the nails in his hands and hung him on a cross. Can you think of situations, either in personal life or society at large, where forgiveness would be the inappropriate thing to do? If so, how can you reconcile those cases with Jesus' statement?

5. Can you think of ways in which some of Jesus' other megatruths might, at times, override his teaching about forgiveness? For example, is forgiveness and pardon always the loving thing to do in all situations?

6. The current world peace movement has undoubtedly built its thinking on this megatruth. List the values and hazards of applying this principle on a world scale.

7. Are there any ways in which you feel our local church should make greater application of this megatruth? Are there ways you need to apply it more in your personal life?

Additional Examples

Jesus says the peacemakers will be blessed. (Matthew 5:9)

Jesus says we should make friends with our accusers. (Matthew 5:21–26 and Luke 12:57–59)

The point of the prodigal son parable is actually *repentance* and God's continual seeking of those who lack the ability to find him, but Jesus also highlights a God who forgives in the same way Jesus urges people to forgive. (Luke 15:11–32)

16

Extroversion Unlimited

A retired army general and his wife joined a church in Melbourne, Florida, soon after moving there. During the two years that followed, this couple was instrumental in bringing eighteen friends and acquaintances into the membership of that congregation.

A Gallup Poll Youth Survey shows that the percentage of teenagers who say they have tried to encourage someone to believe in Jesus Christ or accept him as Savior during the past week has increased significantly since 1977. The number of adults who engage in this type of activity has increased by even greater proportion.

In 1811, the first American missionaries arrived in China. U.S. churches funded this work so generously that their ranks grew rapidly in the latter half of that century. By 1925, 8,000 missionaries were working in China.

Billy Graham and his associates have drawn large attendances and strong financial support for their crusades for more than three decades. Countless other efforts, like the "church growth movement" centered in Pasadena, California, have received good support for similar goals using slightly different methods.

The thinking and actions in each of these examples grows out of another of Jesus' twenty megatruths: *Entering God's kingdom gives you the desire to help other people enter it, too.* Here are a few examples: "Go therefore and make disciples of all nations, baptizing them in the name of the Father and of the Son and of the Holy Spirit, and teaching them to obey everything that I have commanded you" (Matthew 28:19–20). In Matthew 18:10–14, he tells a parable about the urgent need to find one lost sheep even though ninety-nine are safe in the fold. In Matthew 9:36–38 he speaks of sending workers to ripe harvest fields. In Mark 16:15, he gives the clear imperative to preach the gospel all over the world. In Luke 15:1–32, he says we should as eagerly seek to communicate with people about God's kingdom as we would seek to find a lost coin, a lost sheep, or a lost son.

The Dominicans, a Spanish monastic order founded by St. Dominic in 1215, paid much attention to this megatruth and ultimately extended themselves into all the countries of Europe. Their preachers went everywhere to strengthen the faith of believers and oppose the growing tendencies to "heresy" of which in later times they became known as the fiercest persecutors.

MEGATRUTH SIXTEEN

Entering God's kingdom gives you the desire to help other people enter it, too.

The monastic Order of Jesuits, established in 1534 by a Spaniard named Ignatius Loyola, have also used a strong proselytizing emphasis. Fighting the Protestant Reformation as a counterrevolutionary force, they were suppressed by law for a time and even by the pope himself in 1773. But in later centuries, they reappeared as one of the most potent forces for spreading and strengthening the Roman Catholic Church throughout the world. It was largely through efforts of the Jesuits that all the native races of South America, Mexico, and Canada were converted. Because of them, Roman Catholic missions came to heathen lands centuries ahead of

Protestant missionaries, thus greatly increasing the numerical supremacy of the Catholic Church in those nations today.

The Moravians, a small sect group from which John Wesley got some of his greatest spiritual insights, worked hard in the establishment of foreign missions as early as 1732. Their people were sent to Asia, Greenland, the Native-Americans, and the blacks of the West Indies. In proportion to its tiny membership at home, no other denomination has maintained as many foreign missions throughout their history.

In more modern times, the strong missionary emphasis of the Presbyterian, Methodist, and Baptist groups in the late nineteenth and early twentieth centuries leaned heavily on this megatruth. Some small denominations, like the Christian and Missionary Alliance Church, make this megatruth their main work, pouring much money into personnel and mission stations to see it accomplished.

Parachurch networks such as Young Life, Teen Challenge, and Campus Crusade have focused on a similar goal among youth and college students in the U.S. since World War II.

God doesn't call many of us to be lawyers, but he has subpoenaed all of us as witnesses.

Discovery Questions for Group Discussion

1. Read Luke 15:1–32. Using these parables of the lost sheep, the lost coin, and the lost son, Jesus illustrates the great value God places on helping persons enter the new level of consciousness that he called the kingdom of God. Jesus is obviously speaking here of persons who are presently outside the Jewish religious tradition. His primary point is not the need for a repentant attitude. The lost coin and the lost sheep did not repent; they were found because of a "seeking attitude" on the part of their owners.

These three parables were one of the ways Jesus tried to help the Jews see that God was interested in persons outside their small circle. In what ways does their attitude of disinterest toward the Gentiles remind you of attitudes common among American church members today? In what ways is it different?

After reflecting on this text, list some different "types" of persons in our community about whom you feel God will rejoice when they enter his kingdom.

2. Read John 3:17. Jesus says that he came to help people rather than condemn them. Give as many biblical illustrations as you remember of times when he reached out to people in order to do that.

3. Read Luke 5:1–11 (also found in Matthew 4:19 and Mark 1:17). Illustrate all the ways you can think of by which Christians can presently live out Jesus' prediction in this text.

4. Read Matthew 9:36–38 (also found in Luke 10:1–2). What did Jesus mean by these statements?

5. Read Matthew 28:19–20 (also found in Mark 16:15–18; Luke 24:45–49; and John 21:4–22). This text is called the great commission. List the ways our local church fulfills this commission.

6. Read John 20:21. Do you think the statement in this text applies to Christians today? If so, exactly where does Jesus send us? Studies show that 70 to 90 percent of all persons who join any church are friends, relatives, or acquaintances of people who already belong to that church. Take three minutes of silence and see if you can list the names of three acquaintances who don't presently attend a church.

7. Read Acts 1:3–8. In what ways do you think our sending of missionaries to distant lands has become a

substitute for practicing the recommendation in this text closer to home?

8. Do you think it is possible to carry this megatruth too far? Illustrate.

9. Do you think some Christians tend to disregard this megatruth completely? Illustrate.

10. Would society in general suffer any detrimental effects if all Christians stopped living by this megatruth?

11. In what ways do you think Christians best find a balance between evangelistic fanaticism and evangelistic neglect?

Additional Examples

Jesus is criticized by the religious authorities and responds that he has come to call sinners, not the righteous. (Mark 2:15–17 and Luke 5:29–32)

Jesus reaches out to help a despised tax collector enter the kingdom and says he came to seek and save the lost. (Luke 19:1–10)

Jesus says he has come to preach the good news of the kingdom to many cities. (Luke 4:42–44 and Mark 1:35–39)

Jesus says that John the Baptist is a messenger to prepare the way for the kingdom. (Matthew 11:9–10 and Luke 7:26–27)

John the Baptist helps two disciples see that Jesus is the anointed one of the kingdom. One of them, Andrew, helps Peter see this, also. Then Philip introduces Nathanael to Jesus. (John 1:35–42, 44–46)

Jesus says he has appointed the disciples so that they can go and bear much fruit. (John 15:8, 16)

Jesus says the disciples will bear witness to him because they have been with him since the beginning. (John 15:27)

Jesus says in a prayer that he has sent the disciples into the world as God has sent him. (John 17:18)

Jesus sends out the Twelve to reach others. (Matthew 10:1–8; Mark 6:7; and Luke 9:1–2)

Jesus tells Ananias and Paul that Paul will be sent to be a witness to the Gentiles, the kings, and the sons of Israel. (Acts 9:1–19; 22:6–21; 23:11; 26:14–18)

Jesus appears to Paul in Corinth and tells him not to be afraid to teach and preach. (Acts 18:1–11)

Jesus says we are to let our lights shine. (Matthew 5: 14–16)

17

Don't Rob Yourself!

A lawyer in Decatur, Illinois, was called to Washington in 1941 to help the Roosevelt administration with the war effort. After the war, he traveled across the nation helping raise money to establish "Radio Free Europe." George was forever involved in a project to help someone, either on a national or individual scale. After returning to Illinois, he brought a European refugee family into his home and helped them get established in a job. He dried out several alcoholics by giving them work on his farm and getting them involved in Alcoholics Anonymous. Some of his farmer neighbors made fun of George. Because he concentrated more on kindness than agriculture, his farming practices were often careless. His unselfishness bought him many problems. Many of the people he helped took advantage of him. But in spite of this, George was one of the happiest people you could meet.

Down the road from George Fulk lived another man we shall call Joe Green. If a trophy had been awarded for the most selfish person on earth, he would have won it. He lived for his farm, and only his farm. He never went anywhere. He never "traded work" with his neighbors: That might obligate him. He never loaned any of his machinery to anyone:

108

They might damage it. Joe was so tight with money that the neighbors said he squeaked when he walked. For Joe, everything had a dollar sign on it. His brother stayed overnight with him once and asked to borrow Joe's electric razor the next morning. He had forgotten his. After using it, he kiddingly asked Joe what he owed him for rent on the razor. Joe said, "About a nickel, I suppose." But Joe wasn't kidding. His brother paid it, and Joe took it. Joe was a good farmer and was respected for that by his neighbors. But they also knew that Joe was one of the most miserable men on earth. He was anxious and critical, always afraid someone would try to take something from him or that he might lose some money and come to financial ruin.

These two neighbors illustrate another of Jesus' important teachings: People who develop the habit of giving themselves unselfishly find a level of meaning in life that others miss. Those who concentrate on protecting and preserving themselves often do that, but that is all they do. John Wesley

MEGATRUTH SEVENTEEN

If you want to enter God's kingdom, you must live a self-giving life.

said people who have poor giving habits rob God. Jesus went beyond that. He said people with poor giving habits rob themselves.

Megatruth Number Seventeen: *If you want to enter God's kingdom, you must live a self-giving life.* Examples: "It is more blessed to give than to receive" (Acts 20:35). "If any want to become my followers, let them deny themselves and take up their cross and follow me" (Matthew 16:24). In Matthew 20:26–28, Jesus says that the person who wants to be greatest among his followers must be the servant of all other servants. In Mark 12:41–44, he uses the story of a widow's penny to illustrate the virtue of extreme sacrifice. In Matthew 10:16–25, he says that entering God's kingdom will bring some people into persecution and a need for making sacrifices. In Luke 17:7–10, he pictures the self-giving servant who does his duty as a model disciple.

Living into this megatruth feeds one of the deepest hungers of human life. Without it, we become emotionally and spiritually emaciated. Self-preservation is a necessary and natural human instinct, but too much of it is self-destructive. You can play it so close to the chest that you hug yourself to death. That is what happened to the man in Jesus' parable who went and hid his talent in the ground (Matthew 25:14–30).

Charles Kemp, a distinguished professor of pastoral counseling, once said in a sermon that the three greatest maxims in the world are:

"Know thyself"—Socrates of Athens
"Control thyself"—Marcus Aurelius of Rome
"Give thyself"—Jesus of Nazareth

In the somewhat hyper-psychologized "me generation" of the 1970s we concentrated much on "know thyself" and often belittled efforts to "control thyself." In this navel-gazing self-absorption, we began to suffer amnesia regarding "give thyself." Recovering the balance in these three helps our mental health in ways that focusing on the first one, alone, can never do.

A commitment to self-giving is also the energizing force behind some of the world's greatest Christian accomplishments. The Franciscans, a monastic order founded in 1209 by St. Francis of Assisi, were established on this megatruth. Spreading rapidly over all Europe, they became the most numerous of all the orders. During the Black Death, a pestilence that swept through Europe in the fourteenth century, more than 124,000 Franciscan monks perished while ministering to the dying and dead. The prison movement started by Charles Colson, the former "hatchet man" for Richard Nixon who went to prison for Watergate-related offenses, was powered by this determination to give of self to a worthy cause. Much of the world's philanthropic work grows out of this megatruth. Financial giving is seldom motivated solely by the need for money to support a worthy cause. It also rests on the giver's instinctive need to break through the iron cage of self-centeredness. At the heart of financial commitment is the intuition that life's deepest meanings lie in finding a commitment outside ourselves. Our inner urge toward self-giving was illustrated in the enormous public response to a call for Peace Corps volunteers during the 1960s. That—and the volunteering of Christians to similar great causes throughout the centuries—signals the startling news that churches may be asking too little of people rather than too much. In discussing the idealism of contemporary youth, someone observed that the cults are the promissory notes the church never paid. Young people, often sensing Jesus' accuracy better than their parents', seek an ultimate significance to which they can give their lives. When a cult leader demands total commitment, they are often ready to respond. The challenge is big enough to solicit their attention and their lives.

In the nineteenth-century era of Christian missionary expansion to the far corners of the globe, young people sailed away for the unknown, knowing that more than half would die before returning home, knowing that they would bury some of their children in a strange land. Why did they go? Because of the good they could do for others? Yes, but also because they knew Jesus was right: Self-giving can be more important than life itself. If we don't respond to the call for self-giving, we can miss experiencing life while traveling through it. When that happens, life can end long before we die. Robert Frost describes that common disaster in two lines from his poem "The Death of the Hired Man":

> Nothing to look backward to with pride,
> And nothing to look forward to with hope.

During the 1980s, students entered full-time study at Springdale College in Birmingham, England, with the full awareness that their denomination did not have a single church in England large enough to pay a full-time salary. Some resigned good jobs to prepare for ministry at a time when England's unemployment rate was 13.5 percent. Yet, few of them felt they were doing something heroic. On the contrary, they were getting more than they were giving because they were beginning to experience the deep meaning that comes to people who respond to God's call for self-giving.

David Livingstone opened up Africa to Christianity. He walked across it from both directions, making maps as he went. During many of those years, he was out of touch with the outside world. On one such occasion, he received a letter containing this inquiry: "Have you found a good road to where you are? If so, we want to know how to send other men to join you." Livingstone wrote back, "If you have men who will come only if they know there is a good road, I don't want them. I want men who will come if there is no road at all." That is the kind of commitment Jesus asks from each of his followers. Those unwilling to give it have difficulty finding the door to his kingdom.

A cartoon depicted a Gothic-style door that readers could instantly see was the entrance to a church. A sign in the middle of the door said, "Servants' Entrance."

Those who enter God's kingdom go through a similar door.

Discovery Questions for Group Discussion

1. Read Matthew 20:20–22 and Matthew 20:25–28 (also found in Mark 10:35–39, 41–45 and Luke 22:24–27). Jesus says that those who enter his new level of consciousness will want to serve as he has served. Do you recall feeling an increased desire to help and serve other people at the time you first became a Christian? If so, has that feeling stayed at a constant level over the years, or does it rise and fall? Make a list of factors that you think tend to increase our desire to serve others.

2. Read Mark 9:33–35. Jesus seems to say that those who enter his kingdom most fully are those who most fully give themselves in serving others. Have you had life experiences (times when you were intensely engaged in helping others) that seem to validate that teaching?

3. Read Matthew 10:38 and Matthew 16:24 (also found in Luke 9:23; 14:27 and Mark 8:34). The text indicates that a cross is not some life problem or burden that "chooses us"; it is some task that we *voluntarily choose* as a way of serving God and other people. We know that individuals can do this, but are there ways in which a church or a government sometimes chooses to do the same thing?

4. Read Luke 12:32–34. Jesus urges the disciples to concentrate on self-giving rather than on the getting of possessions. Isn't it possible to do both things at once? For example, don't some people in the medical field who make high incomes also concentrate on giving themselves in service to other people?

5. Read Matthew 10:37 (also found in Luke 14:25–26). Jesus says that we cannot enter the kingdom unless we give it a higher priority than our family. What do you think he means by this statement?

6. Read John 13:1–17. Jesus washes the disciples' feet in order to demonstrate that they are to serve others as he has served them. Name some individuals who you feel have lived that kind of lifestyle.

7. List some ways contemporary church members can practice this megatruth.

8. Do you think some contemporary churches carry this megatruth to extremes? If so, illustrate.

9. What additional opportunities for self-giving do you feel your local congregation should offer its members?

Additional Examples

Jesus praises the poor widow whose giving of all she had revealed that her self-giving came from the heart. (Mark 12:41–44 and Luke 21:1–4)

Jesus says those whose self-giving leads them to persecution are blessed. (Matthew 5:10–11 and Luke 6:22–23)

Using the analogy of a man who begins to build a tower, Jesus says we must count the cost of entering the kingdom, for it will be great. (Luke 14:28–30)

Using the analogy of a king who goes to war, Jesus says we must count the great cost of entering the kingdom. (Luke 14:31–33)

Using the analogy of the servant who works hard in the field and then prepares supper, Jesus says those who enter the kingdom will feel positive about doing what God calls them to do. (Luke 17:7–10)

Jesus praises the strength and commitment of John the Baptist. (Matthew 11:7–8)

Jesus says he has no place to lay his head. (Matthew 8:19–20 and Luke 9:57–58)

Jesus says that people hate him because he tells the truth about what is evil. (John 7:1–9)

Jesus says he is like a good shepherd who lays down his life for his sheep. (John 10:11–18)

Jesus asks the Jews why they are preparing to stone him. (John 10:31–32)

Jesus says he must give his life for the kingdom. (John 12:23–24, 27–28, 33)

Jesus says he must give his life, though he is tempted to withhold it. (Matthew 16:21–23; Mark 8:31–33; and Luke 9:21–22)

Jesus says he will be killed and rise on the third day. (Matthew 17:22–23; 20:17–19; 26:1–2; Mark 9:30–32; 10:32–34; and Luke 9:43–45; 18:31–34)

Jesus predicts that his closest disciples will fall away while he gives his life. (Mark 14:26–31; Luke 22:31–34; and John 13:36–38)

Jesus voluntarily gives himself to his executioners. (Matthew 26:47–56; Mark 14:43–50; Luke 22:35–38, 47–53; and John 18:1–11, 19–24; 19:11)

Jesus feels forsaken by God in his self-giving on the cross. (Matthew 27:46 and Mark 15:34)

As Jesus begins his ministry and travels to Galilee, he says to Philip, "Follow me." (John 1:43)

Jesus calls Matthew to follow him. (Matthew 9:9; Mark 2:13–14; and Luke 5:27–32)

Jesus says his followers should leave the dead to bury the dead. (Matthew 8:21–22 and Luke 9:59–60)

Jesus urges the disciples to follow him in self-giving. (John 21:4–22)

Jesus says those who find eternal life must hate their life in this world, follow him, and serve him. (John 12:25)

A disciple will be maligned as his teacher was. (Matthew 10:24–25 and Luke 6:39–40)

Jesus says he has not come to bring peace. (Matthew 10:34–37; Luke 12:49–53; and Mark 13:12–13)

Jesus says the disciples, like himself, will make the sacrifice of being hated for the kingdom's sake. (John 15:18–25; 16:1–4)

Jesus predicts that brother will deliver brother to death because of the kingdom. (Matthew 10:21–22)

Jesus tells the disciples that they will be brought to judgment before councils. (Matthew 10:16–18)

Jesus tells Ananias and Paul that Paul will suffer greatly in his work as a witness. (Acts 9:1–19; 22:6–21; 23:11)

18

Severed Branches Wilt

A hiker got lost in the woods. For hours he circled in the tangled underbrush, vainly seeking a landmark. Everywhere he turned, masses of unfamiliar greenery increased his confusion. Finally, just as the sun was setting, he stumbled through a bramble thicket onto a broad highway. Instantly, he knew where he was. He still had a long walk ahead, but in a sense he had already arrived. He had his bearings. He had the feeling of home in his head.

Walking into God's kingdom brings that kind of feeling. This does not, however, mean a hiker will never be tempted to take a shortcut and get lost again. Entering the kingdom is not like boarding the Concorde for a nonstop flight to London. In that experience, you lose your freedom of choice. Getting lost is not an option. The crew will not let you get off the plane in midair. Entering God's kingdom is more like finding the right road—while retaining the personal freedom to wander off it before you get home.

The term "saved" does not describe *every aspect* of our relationship with God. "Given away" is another important part of it. We are not just saved from lostness like a dime picked up in the street by a pedestrian. We *decide* to give ourselves away to the right road home. God does not chain us to his kingdom. After giving ourselves to his level of consciousness, we retain the freedom to repossess ourselves back into a self-centered lostness. Entering the kingdom does not guarantee that we will stay there—anymore than entering the door of a fine new home means we will continue to live in it. The old argument of "once in Grace, always in Grace" does not go far enough. It deals with only one part of our Christian experience. We certainly do not leave God's grace (his love and forgiveness), but entering the kingdom involves more than just God's side of the transaction. We enter it with a changed heart (see Megatruth Number Two). We can leave it the same way. The kingdom has exit lanes as well as entrance lanes.

Megatruth Number Eighteen: *If your thinking and actions become self-centered, you can disconnect from God's kingdom.* Examples: "No one who puts a hand to the plow and looks back is fit for the kingdom of God" (Luke 9:62). "Whoever does not abide in me is thrown away like a branch and withers; such branches are gathered, thrown into the fire, and burned" (John 15:6). "Not everyone who says to me, 'Lord, Lord,' will enter the kingdom of heaven, but only the one who does the will of my Father in heaven" (Matthew 7:21). Jesus illustrates in Matthew 7:15–27 the need for *continued* right attitudes and actions by saying that a tree is known by its fruits, and by telling a story of two different kinds of house builders. In Matthew 21:33–45, he tells a parable about tenant farmers who reap the reward of unfaithfulness in their vineyard work. In Matthew 25:14–30, the parable of invested and uninvested money illustrates the need to act in faithful service, or lose the opportunity to participate in the kingdom experience. In Matthew 25:31–46, the parable of sheep and goats illustrates the need to act out the experience of the kingdom in order to avoid losing it.

MEGATRUTH EIGHTEEN

If your thinking and actions become self-centered, you can disconnect from God's kingdom.

Jesus everywhere says that we must live the truth as well as hear it. Living the truth involves making the outside behavior match the interior feelings and attitudes. Unless that happens, the resulting division splits us from the kingdom we are trying to experience.

Few new denominations hang their basic theology on this hook, but this teaching is often stressed by groups that place a high premium on "good works" or following certain religious legalisms. Loyal members of sects or small denominations that emphasize tithing, feet washing, or baptism by certain precise formulas are particularly tempted to insist that their pet religious practice is a prerequisite for salvation and eternal life.

Although we cannot and should not try to *judge* whether people are in or out of the kingdom (see Megatruth Number Fourteen regarding the need for nonjudgmental attitudes), we can identify some of the ways they begin drifting off the road. One of these involves the substitution of talk for action. Twin brothers grew up, went away to school, and eventually settled in the same town. One was a minister and the other a physician. People were always getting the twins confused. One day, a man stopped one of them on the street and said, "I want to compliment you on that inspiring sermon you preached last Sunday." The doctor replied with, "You have us mixed up. I'm not the brother who preaches; I'm the one who practices." When Jesus compared the actions of the priest and Levite to that of the Good Samaritan on the Jericho Road, he was noting that not everyone who preaches, practices.

This danger of substituting kingdom talk for kingdom behavior is difficult to avoid because we can do it without knowing we are doing it. A woman in Stuttgart, West Germany, had to call for help to revive her husband after she knocked him cold. She told authorities she hit him over the head with a coffee pot when he insisted on watching a violent crime show on TV. "I don't like our children to see any violence in this house," she said.

The ease with which average people are unknowingly inconsistent is reflected in a conversation between a mother and her little girl. "Do you know what happens to little girls who tell lies?" the mother asked. "Of course I do," the child replied. "They grow up and tell their little girls that their hair will be curly if they eat their spinach."

Another way people begin to drift out of the kingdom is by drifting into bad habits. In 1958, William Sloan Coffin, Jr., was chaplain at Yale. He said to one of the seniors, "You're a nice guy. You have lots of charm but little inner strength. And if you don't stand for something, you're apt to fall for anything." Sixteen years later, Jeb Stuart Macgruder stood before a federal bench, a confessed felon from the Watergate epic, and said, "I know what I have done, and your honor knows what I have done....Somewhere between my ambition and my ideals, I lost my ethical compass."

E. Stanley Jones told about a sign he saw at the intersection where a dirt road branched off a highway in Canada. During those decades, cars stood on tall wheels so they could maneuver the mud of unpaved country roads. "Pick your rut with care" the sign read. Habits of thinking and acting that seem unimportant in the beginning often take us places we had not intended to go. If these habit ruts are not consistent with the kingdom level of consciousness, they can gradually drag us out of it.

Another way we can begin to leave the kingdom is by substituting religious ritual for religious behavior. A minister was touring a weaving mill under the guidance of a foreman who was one of his church members. Mentioning the name of another church member who worked there, he said he assumed John was one of their best weavers. "I'm sorry to say that he isn't," the foreman said. "John is always standing around talking about his religion when he ought to be tending to his loom. He needs to learn that when he is at work his religion ought to come out through his fingers, not his mouth."

A man bought a pair of shoes that had a beautiful plaid lining. He felt elegant each time he put them on, but no one else ever saw the lining. Jesus said that religion can be beautiful on the inside but invisible at the office on Monday morning. This was his main criticism of the ritually pure Pharisees. He said that a religion that is vital, is visible. When Peter suggested on the Mount of Transfiguration that they build tabernacles there, Jesus immediately led them back to their work among the people. He never succumbed to the subtle danger of substituting right ritual for right actions (Matthew 17:1–13).

Another way we can begin to drift out of the kingdom is by losing our communication with God. Many years ago, an NBC affiliate radio station got a letter from a prospector in Montana. He wrote, "I am a regular listener to your programs, and I want to ask you a favor. It gets lonely up here. Except for my piano and my dog, I don't have much company. I do have a violin I used to play, but since the piano is now so badly out of tune, I can't tune the violin anymore. Would you please be kind enough at seven o'clock next Sunday night to strike me an 'A' so I can put my fiddle back in tune?" The station interrupted their regular programming to comply with his request. We stay in tune with God through a number of means—worship, daily prayer, Bible study, and fellowship with others of like mind. Without these aids, we drift off the road and out of tune. Not because God takes his grace away from us. Because we take our *self* away from him.

A wife tugged at her husband's sleeve as she pointed across a large crowd at a church convention. "That looks like Fred," she said.

"Yes, it does," her husband replied. "But then, a lot of people can look like a lot of things they are not."

Discovery Questions for Group Discussion

1. Read Matthew 5:13 (also found in Luke 14:34–35). When Jesus says that salt can become worthless, he is undoubtedly referring to the persons in the Beatitude

verses just above who previously had been willing to make sacrifices for the kingdom but lost that commitment. Have you known persons who seemed to fit that description? What do you think caused them to change?

2. Read Luke 9:61–62. Jesus says that persons who turn back from the commitments called for in his new level of consciousness block themselves from continuing in it. Later in the New Testament, Paul says our entry is a gift from God and not by our own efforts. How do you reconcile these two ideas?

3. Read Matthew 7:21–23 (also found in Luke 6:46). Jesus says that words alone (without the doing of God's will) cannot keep us in his level of consciousness. Make a list of the actions that you feel are absolutely essential for continuing in that experience.

4. Read John 15:2 and John 15:6. Jesus says that God removes branches that bear no fruit. Some people think that is true of entire denominations (such as those that have been shrinking numerically during the past twenty years). What do you think? Why?

5. Read Matthew 5:29–30 and Matthew 18:7–9 (also found in Mark 9:43–50). Jesus says that our actions can pull us back outside the kingdom. Some denominations teach that once an individual achieves spiritual wholeness (salvation), this can never be lost. How do you reconcile these two seemingly opposite ideas?

6. Read Matthew 6:13 (also found in Luke 11:4). Jesus prays in this verse from the Lord's Prayer that God not lead us into temptation. Does this mean God sets up situations in which we are tempted to drift out of his level of consciousness?

7. Do you feel contemporary churches have neglected this megatruth? Illustrate your opinion.

8. Do you think some contemporary churches carry this megatruth to extremes?

Additional Examples

Jesus says those who hunger for righteousness will be blessed. (Matthew 5:6)

Jesus says those who are pure in heart will be blessed. (Matthew 5:8)

Jesus says the kingdom will be taken away from the Jews and given to those who produce its fruits. (Matthew 21:33–46)

Jesus illustrates by his parable of the soils that people can get a taste of the kingdom and then leave it. (Matthew 13:20–21; Mark 4:13–17; and Luke 8:12–13)

Jesus uses the story of a man who built his house on sand to illustrate that doing his words about the kingdom is more important than *hearing* his words. (Matthew 7:24–27 and Luke 6:47–49)

Jesus says that bad trees which do not bear fruit are thrown into the fire. (Matthew 7:15–20)

Jesus says he who finds his life (in self-centeredness) will lose it. (Matthew 10:39; 16:25; Luke 9:24; and Mark 8:35)

Jesus warns the disciples against doing things with their eyes (minds), hands, or feet which will rule them out of the kingdom. (Mark 9:43–48)

Jesus recognizes that some disciples, even one of the twelve inner circle, are not able to continue their belief in him. (John 6:66–71)

Jesus says he will deny before God whoever denies him before other people. (Matthew 10:33; 16:27; Mark 8:38; and Luke 12:9–10)

19

Hell Is Homemade

Is there a hell? Who goes there? Why? What is it like? Few questions generate greater disagreement among religious people.

Jonathan Edwards, a Boston minister in the 1700s, preached a famous sermon entitled "Sinners in the Hands of an Angry God." Eyewitnesses said some parishioners were so terrified by his words that they hid under their pews, shaking with fear.

Much contemporary thinking runs to the opposite extreme. Few church members could be frightened by such a sermon today. Angry, perhaps, but not scared. Most of them would consider it uncouth, unnecessary, unbiblical, and perhaps even unchristian. They do not believe God operates like a stern old judge who raps his gavel down on our fingers for making mistakes. A California TV guru, Terry Cole-Whittaker, communicates this "God is a good ol' boy" theory in a mixture of religion and pop psychology. "God loves me, and God would never send me to hell, because it doesn't exist," she tells her La Jolla congregation. She says hell is a state of mind and human sin is an outmoded concept. "I don't believe everybody is lost, because everybody gets to make it," she says. "Heaven is a cinch."

Dietrich Bonhoeffer, the German pastor-theologian who died in a Nazi prison, called this contemporary trend "Cheap Grace." He labeled as unbiblical the view that God forgives just about everybody for just about anything just about anytime, even if they never admit they are wrong and ask for forgiveness.

These arguments can go on forever—and probably will. But while we may honestly disagree about the concept of hell, we cannot deny that Jesus taught about a judgment of this sort in the strongest possible terms. Megatruth Number Nineteen: *Failing to enter God's kingdom brings you negative results.* Examples: "So it will be at the end of the age. The angels will come out and separate the evil from the righteous and throw them into the furnace of fire, where there will be weeping and gnashing of teeth" (Matthew 13:49–50). In Jesus' wheat and weeds parable of Matthew 13:24–30, 36–43, the weeds are eventually burned up. In Matthew 23:29–36, he describes the punishment of the Pharisees who refuse to enter God's kingdom. In Matthew 24:45–51, he pictures the dire fate of an unfaithful servant. In Luke 16:19–31, he contrasts the extreme opposite

MEGATRUTH NINETEEN

Failing to enter God's kingdom brings you negative results.

fates of the rich man and Lazarus. In Luke 10:13–16, he paints a black day for the towns that didn't believe in him. In John 5:19–29, he plainly says that the unsaved are damned.

Fundamentalists and superconservative sects that emerge from already conservative denominations often emphasize this teaching, using the fear of hell as a bludgeon to motivate conversions. Many preachers in more liberal denominations have used this teaching in a different way. They, too, contrast the positive results of a relationship with God with the negative consequences of not relating. But they say these positive and negative outcomes are reaped in the here and now, not later in hell or heaven.

Ministers who believe the penalty for not entering the kingdom comes primarily in the present life emphasize this kind of illustration: A man built a new house and wanted to surround it with a beautiful lawn. He worked hard to level the soil and planted it to grass. He was feeling great until the seed came up. He had planted the whole yard to lettuce by mistake. This is what many people feel the Carpenter means by the judgment of God—an impersonal principle that operates as systematically as the law of gravity. If you jump out a ten-story window, you fall down, not up. If you live your life self-centeredly (outside the circle of God-consciousness), you will be in deep trouble—not after you die, but immediately. In other words, you reap what you sow, and you don't have to wait forty years to know it is lettuce.

Ministers who believe the penalty for not entering the kingdom comes primarily after death emphasize illustrations like this one: Someone asked, "How can I tell the difference between mushrooms and toadstools?" Someone else replied, "Eat some right before you go to bed. If you wake up next morning, they're mushrooms." If you pursue one kind of life, you wake up in one place. If you live another kind of life, you wake up in another kind of place. This view says the eternal punishment for self-centeredly refusing to relate to God is to lose the freedom of choosing to relate to God— forever.

Whatever view you choose, Jesus clearly says the penalty for a self-centered refusal to enter God's level of consciousness is homemade. It is not something God does to us. We build it for ourselves.

An old story tells about a wealthy man who called in a trusted assistant who had been working for him thirty years. "Jim," he said, "I am leaving for a trip around the world. I'll be gone for about ten months. While I'm gone, I want you to build a house for me. Here are the blueprints, and here is a check for $150,000 to cover the cost. I want you to have it completed when I get back." The assistant saw a chance to make some money without hurting anyone. The old man wouldn't need the house long anyway, so he hired a crooked contractor and wherever possible used inferior material. When the house was finished, its beautiful appearance covered shoddy workmanship. The first day after the employer returned, he wanted to see the house. They drove out to it and stepped out of the car. The old man was impressed. "Well, Jim, you may have wondered why I had you build this, since I already have a nice home."

"Yes, I must admit I did," Jim said.

"You have been a faithful employee for many years, Jim, and I wanted to express my appreciation." Handing Jim the house keys, he said, "Here, the house is yours."

> To every man there openeth
> A Way, and Ways, and a Way...
> And every man decideth
> The way his soul shall go.
> —John Oxenham

Discovery Questions for Group Discussion

1. Read Matthew 22:1–14. Jesus says that persons who do not respond to God's call to the new level of consciousness will be punished. Do you think this punishment comes only in life after death? Give reasons for your opinion.

2. Read John 3:18–20. Jesus says that persons who do not believe in him are condemned. This is one of the statements on which Christians who feel it is essential to evangelize people in other world religions base their convictions. What do you think?

3. Read Luke 6:24–26. Jesus predicts woe for those whose preoccupation with money, self-righteousness, and religious pride keeps them from seeking and entering the kingdom. Are there ways in which this sometimes applies to entire nations or whole communities?

4. Read Matthew 13:47–50. Jesus says the kingdom is like a net from which bad fish are removed and burned. Many people cannot reconcile this idea with Jesus' teaching about a forgiving, loving God. What do you think?

5. Read Luke 13:6–9. Jesus says that those who do not enter the kingdom will be "cut down." How important do you think it is for contemporary churches to preach this idea?

6. In what ways do you think contemporary churches have tended to neglect this megatruth?

7. Are there ways in which you think some contemporary churches have carried this megatruth too far?

8. Some contemporary Christian leaders feel that the preaching of this megatruth to our generation drives people away from the kingdom rather than attracting them toward it. What do you think?

Additional Examples

Jesus says in the parable of the wheat and tares that the weeds will be burned. (Matthew 13:30, 40–42)

Jesus says those who make excuses for not entering the kingdom will be punished. (Luke 14:15–24)

Jesus says many who appear to be first now will be last at the final coming of the kingdom. (Matthew 19:30; 20:16; and Luke 13:30)

Jesus says all must repent in order to avoid punishment for not entering the kingdom. (Luke 13:1–5)

Jesus says many will seek to enter but will not be able. (Luke 13:22–27)

Using the parable of a rich man and Lazarus, Jesus predicts dire consequences in hell for those who do not respond to the kingdom. (Luke 16:19–31)

Jesus says those who have done evil will be judged at the end time. (John 5:29)

Jesus says those who love their life will lose it. (John 12:25)

In his parable of the great feast, Jesus warns that those who do not respond to the kingdom will not taste it. (Luke 14:15–24)

Jesus says that on the day of judgment, people will render account for every careless word. (Matthew 12:36–37)

Jesus says God cannot forgive us if we do not forgive others. (Matthew 18:23–35)

Jesus says speaking against the power of the Holy Spirit will not be forgiven. (Mark 3:28–30; Matthew 12:30–32; and Luke 11:23)

Jesus says that casting your pearls before swine (fixing your attention in the wrong direction) will destroy you. (Matthew 7:6)

Jesus says those who take great pride in their religious practices will be punished. (Matthew 23:11–12)

Jesus says those who prevent people from entering the kingdom by leading them astray into religious ritual will be punished. (Matthew 23:13–15)

Jesus says the religious leaders who do not enter the kingdom will be punished severely. (Matthew 23:29–36 and Luke 11:45–52)

Jesus says the Jerusalem religious leaders will be punished because they did not recognize the kingdom. (Matthew 23:37–38; 24:1–2; Luke 13:31–35; 19:41–44; and Mark 13:1–2)

Jesus warns the Pharisees that they will die in their sins if they do not believe in him. (John 8:21–24)

The people in Jesus' hometown do not receive healing because they cannot accept the idea that such a familiar person could have this power. (Mark 6:1–6; Luke 4:16–30; and Matthew 13:53–58)

Jesus says many sons of the kingdom (descendants of Abraham and Isaac) will be thrown into outer darkness. (Matthew 8:12 and Luke 13:28)

Jesus says woe will come to Chorazin and Bethsaida, because they did not repent. (Matthew 11:20–24 and Luke 10:13–15)

Jesus says his generation will be judged harshly for not accepting the kingdom. (Matthew 12:38–42; 16:1–4; Mark 8:11–12; and Luke 11:29–32; 12:54–56)

Jesus says blind guides will fall into a pit. (Matthew 15:12–14)

After driving traders out of the temple, Jesus uses the unproductive fig tree to describe the negatives that will come to the Jewish leaders because of their failure to recognize him and help people find the kingdom. (Matthew 21:17–20 and Mark 11:12–14, 20–21)

Jesus says those who reject him and the kingdom will be punished. (Matthew 21:33–45; Mark 12:1–12; and Luke 20:9–19)

Jesus says those who reject him and his sayings will be judged on the last day. (John 12:47–48)

Jesus says his evil generation will be much worse off for not accepting the kingdom. (Matthew 12:43–45 and Luke 11:24–26)

Jesus predicts dire consequences for the person who betrays him. (Matthew 26:20–25; Mark 14:17–21; Luke 22:21–23; and John 13:21–30; 19:11)

Jesus tells the disciples to shake the dust off their feet in places where people do not listen to them and predicts dire consequences for those persons. (Matthew 10:14–15; Mark 6:11; and Luke 9:5; 10:10–12)

Jesus says it would be better for people to have a millstone placed around their neck than to cause one of his disciples to sin. (Matthew 18:6; Mark 9:42; and Luke 17:1–2)

20

I Shall Return

When General Douglas MacArthur left the Philippine Islands in the early days of World War II, his three-word promise was quoted in newspapers around the world: "I shall return." Jesus said the same thing.

American pastors treat this promise in two opposite ways. Some disregard it altogether. They feel that such an emphasis on future hope can deflect us from grappling with present realities and living out our discipleship in the here and now. That view was well-articulated by the pastor of Los Angeles' Bel-Air Presbyterian Church, which President Ronald Reagan occasionally attended. "I'm so excited about the First Coming, and my circles are talking about how to express a faith authentically in areas of social problems." He says his primary attention is on "the integrity of Christian faith today rather than the signs of the times."

This benign neglect of the Second Coming has some virtue, but also danger. For one thing, it requires that we ignore a number of clear New Testament statements. It can also be an unconscious way of limiting God to an impotent, distant pedestal. If he doesn't have the power to intervene a second time, where did he get the power to come the first time? Not believing he will return can be a subtle way of believing he didn't come the first time *as the Son of God*—but rather came as a great teacher who, like Abe Lincoln, left us with some precepts to use in working things out for ourselves. Many other pastors take a totally opposite view of the Second Coming: They give it strong emphasis. In so doing, they are moving with the majority opinion. Sixty-two percent of Americans believe Jesus will come back to earth as promised in the Bible.[+] The rising tide of this belief during recent years was accelerated by a 1970 best-selling book by Hal Lindsey entitled *The Late Great Planet Earth*. The mood is fueled today by TV pastors like Jerry Falwell who herald millenarian doom for a decadent society and apostate, humanistic churches. Other leaders who work the same side of the street include H. M. S. Richards, whose national radio broadcast "The Voice of Prophecy" opened with a theme song whose chorus said "Jesus Is Coming Again." John Wesley White, an Irish associate evangelist for the Billy Graham association speaking in Minneapolis, gave support to what many believe when he identified earthquakes and world famine as preludes to Christ's return.

He reminded his audience that the Second Coming is "the most emphasized doctrine" in scripture and is a basic teaching of the historic church, being a part of the Apostles' Creed as well as contemporary statements of belief.

This Second Coming emphasis has several obvious virtues. For one thing, it takes scripture seriously. The return of Christ is mentioned 380 times in the New Testament alone. Twenty-three of the twenty-seven books refer to it. It also takes seriously God's power to intervene in human affairs. But this view also holds some dangers. Concentrating on a future divine rescue mission can make us feel more comfortable resting at the oars of our lifeboat—and thus avoid facing our *present*, strengthened by our relationship with God. Authentic Christianity does not rest its case on God's trans-

[+]*Emerging Trends* (March 1984), reporting 1983 survey results.

forming power in the future. It affirms the present presence of a God who can come into negative circumstances of contemporary life with people-transforming and church-transforming power.

Ammunition for both these opposite views about the Second Coming is found in Jesus' words. He spoke of the kingdom in both present and future terms. It began during his ministry, like a seed sown secretly (Mark 4:26) and like a mustard seed, which starts small and quietly grows into a giant tree (Luke 13:18–19). Yet, it is still to come in the future "with power" (Mark 9:1).

Whatever emphasis we decide to give the Second Coming, we cannot avoid its omnipresence among Jesus' words. Megatruth Number Twenty: *God's kingdom will at an unspecified future time become more fully and obviously manifested in the whole of creation.* Examples: "But I tell you, from now on you will see the Son of Man seated at the right hand of Power and coming on the clouds of heaven" (Matthew 26:64). In

MEGATRUTH TWENTY

God's kingdom will at an unspecified future time become more fully and obviously manifested in the whole of creation.

Matthew 24:3–44, Jesus deals extensively with an end time when the kingdom will become apparent and vividly real to all. In Matthew 25, he tells three parables about ten girls and their lamps, a master and servants, and sheep and goats—in order to say that there will be a final curtain on human history in which the kingdom will come visibly. In Luke 21:5–37, he speaks of the temple's destruction at the end of time, earthquakes, battles, and other physical signs of the last days. No matter how the reader interprets these statements, his point cannot be evaded: Heaven and earth will pass away at some future time and will be replaced by a full-blown kingdom of God.

The General Conference of Seventh-Day Adventists can be traced to the Millerite movement of the 1830s and 1840s when William Miller, a Baptist from Vermont, built his following on a deep concern about the Second Coming of Christ.

Preaching and lecturing throughout the northeastern U.S., Miller pulled members out of every denomination. He announced the return of Christ and the end of the world for the year 1843 but died in 1849 with his prophecy embarrassingly unfulfilled. Sects like Miller's that put a date on the end of history have arisen throughout the centuries, but they never grow large. The obvious failure of their basic tenet (as the set date comes and goes past) tends to tarnish their ability to attract more members. Sects which *begin* at this point must therefore move on to a greater breadth of teaching or a shifted emphasis in order to survive.

The Watchtower Bible and Tract Society of New York, Inc., grew from the same teaching soil. But this group was intelligent enough not to predict the page on which the calendar would end. Charles Taze Russell, a Christian Church minister from Pennsylvania, founded the group in the 1870s, with the name "Jehovah's Witnesses" adopted much later, in 1931. Witnesses label the turmoil in the earth since 1914 as a "sign" that the heavenly kingdom is now functioning. They feel it will destroy the wicked in God's war of Armageddon within the lifetime of this generation. The survivors and resurrected dead will then enjoy the promised 1,000-year reign of Christ, during which time paradise will be restored earthwide. On surviving a final test, 144,000 perfected saints will enter an eternity of joyful life under the loving sovereignty of their God, Jehovah. Witnesses believe they must zealously warn the people that Satan's domination of mankind will shortly end in the "great tribulation." They diligently seek to make disciples of and baptize those desirous of entering into God's new order.

Across northern Alabama and Mississippi and southern Tennessee, numerous crosses beside the highway declare that "Jesus Is Coming Soon." Someone has observed that while it is admirable for people to take the time, energy, and money to call this fact to our attention, we have to question whether they mean what they say. The crosses are made of reinforced concrete.

These may, however, be a fitting symbol for contemporary Christians. Expect him to return. He said he would. In the meantime, build your discipleship with concrete and steel. He calls us to accomplish something before he gets here.

Discovery Questions for Group Discussion

1. Read Matthew 10:23, Luke 9:27, and Matthew 16:28 (also found in Mark 9:1). Jesus seems to say to the disciples that he will return and the kingdom will fully come before their death. Some scholars feel he was speaking of the spiritual coming of the kingdom through the Holy Spirit at Pentecost. How would you explain these texts?

2. Read Matthew 23:39 (also found in Luke 13:35). Jesus says that he will return. Many radio preachers base their prophetic broadcasting on statements like this. Do you think that kind of preaching helps contemporary people respond to Christ and his kingdom? Why or why not?

3. Matthew 25:1–46 contains three parables: the parable of the ten maidens and their lamps waiting on the bridegroom, the parable of the talents, and the parable of the sheep and goats being divided when the Son of man returns. Each of these parables illustrates the same point: "Keep awake therefore, for you know neither the day nor the hour" (Matthew 25:13). The parable of the talents and identical concepts are also found in Luke 19:11–27 and John 5:25–29.

   In these parables, Jesus says those who have helped him and those who have not will be judged when the kingdom comes at the end of earthly time. Does that kind of teaching motivate you, personally, to seek his kingdom? Can you think of historical situations in which this kind of statement would motivate people? Give examples.

4. Read Matthew 26:63–64 (also found in Mark 14:61–62 and Luke 22:66–69). Jesus predicts at his trial that he will come in power at some future time. Some denominations preach this idea frequently; others disregard it altogether. How do preachers in your denomination handle this text? Do you think the socioeconomic level of the people served by your congregation and denomination have any bearing on how much this teaching is used? Give reasons for your opinion.

5. Do you think some contemporary churches carry this idea to extremes? Illustrate.

6. What warnings would you want to give persons who give great emphasis to this teaching?

Additional Examples

Jesus says that at a future time beyond death those who have entered his kingdom will enter it more fully and live on a different level than the present physical one. (Luke 20:27–38; Matthew 22:23–33; and Mark 12:18–27)

Jesus says that at a future time no one knows, a time characterized by anguish across the earth, he and the kingdom will fully come. (Luke 21:7–12, 16–36; 17:20–37; 23:27–31; 12:35–48; and Mark 13:3–37)

Jesus tells Nathanael that he will see the heavens opened and God's angels descending on his anointed one. (John 1:51)

Personal Opinion Survey Regarding Jesus' Twenty Megatruths

Please place a check mark beside the items on this list that you believe Jesus stressed most in his teaching.

After making these check marks, please place a circle around the check marks that are more important to you *personally* than Jesus' other teachings.

❑ 1. You experience new ways of thinking and behavior when you enter God's kingdom.

❑ 2. You enter God's kingdom only by a changed attitude of the heart, not by following a list of religious rules.

❑ 3. Concentrating your attention on Christ strengthens your ability to enter and experience God's kingdom in greater fullness.

❑ 4. Prayer strengthens your ability to enter God's kingdom and experience it more fully.

❑ 5. You are blocked from entering God's kingdom unless you turn away from self-centeredness.

❑ 6. Taking pride in your religious achievements makes it difficult to enter God's kingdom.

❑ 7. Financial wealth makes it more difficult for you to enter God's kingdom because your money brings a false sense of power that distracts you from seeking something better.

❑ 8. Though self-concern is not your goal, you receive rich rewards by entering God's kingdom.

❑ 9. Entering God's kingdom gives you a sense of security that comes from believing your personal needs will be taken care of.

❑ 10. Entering God's kingdom releases a new power in your life and thought processes that transcends the normal cause and effect patterns of your environment.

❑ 11. Entering God's kingdom enables you to live joyfully.

❑ 12. If you enter God's kingdom, you will continue to live in that consciousness beyond the time of physical death.

❑ 13. Entering God's kingdom gives you increased love and concern for other people.

❑ 14. Entering God's kingdom makes you less judgmental about other people.

❑ 15. Entering God's kingdom gives you a more forgiving spirit.

❑ 16. Entering God's kingdom gives you the desire to help other people enter it, too.

❑ 17. If you want to enter God's kingdom, you must live a self-giving life.

❑ 18. If your thinking and actions become self-centered, you can disconnect from God's kingdom.

❑ 19. Failing to enter God's kingdom brings you negative results.

❑ 20. God's kingdom will at an unspecified future time become more fully and obviously manifested in the whole of creation.

Instructions for Teacher: After all individuals have completed the marking of their sheets, list on a flipchart or chalkboard the total checks and circles for each of the twenty points by calling for a show of hands on the following questions: "How many put a check mark by teaching number 1?" "How many put a circle around teaching number 2?" Repeat this question for all twenty points.

After listing the total checks and circles on the chalkboard or flip chart, give group members a copy of the annotated list of twenty megatruths found on the next few pages of this appendix. This list contains some of the key statements Jesus made regarding each megatruth. Use the paragraphs below to lead the group in a discussion.

1. Now that you have counted the total number of check marks for each teaching, you know the five favorite teachings of this group. Ask three or four volunteers to share any early childhood experiences or teachings that they feel caused them to check one of these five.

2. Which of these twenty points do you think positive-thinking and self-esteem pastors such as Robert Schuller emphasize? The answers are 8, 9, 10, and 11.

3. Which of these twenty points do you think are emphasized most by pastors in theologically charismatic congregations? The answers are 3, 9, 10, and 11.

4. Which of these twenty items do you think are emphasized most in the preaching of contemporary fundamentalists and evangelicals? The answers are 8, 16, 19, and 20.

5. Which of these twenty points do you think pastors in theologically moderate and liberal denominations emphasize? The answers are 6, 13, 14, and 17.

6. Which of the twenty teachings do you think most pastors in your denomination emphasize?

7. Which of these twenty items do you think were emphasized most in the preaching of Paul as recorded in the New Testament? The answers are 3, 5, 12, and 19.

8. Can you see how this "theological selectivity" or "biblical fingerprinting" illustrates the following?

- Differences among denominations. If you give this test to Sunday school classes in five different denominations, you will become immediately aware of their dissimilar patterns.
- Differences among pastors in the same denomination.
- Differences between congregations in the same denomination.
- Differences between different generations—1900 to 1940, 1940 to 1965, and 1965 to the present.
- Differences between contemporary sermons and those preached in earlier decades.

9. In what ways would each of us benefit from a more balanced understanding of what Jesus said?

10. In what ways would our class, group, and congregation benefit from overcoming the tendency to concentrate on Jesus' teachings that have been significant for us personally?

If you desire, use the exercise in all adult classes. Reproduce the totals from each of the classes and share them with all the other adult classes the following week. This will tell you whether the older and younger generations in your church share the same or differing theological viewpoints.

A pastor may also find it beneficial to see how his or her theological views compare with those of the different age groups in the church.

Annotated List of Jesus' Twenty Megatruths

How to Enter God's Kingdom

1. *You experience new ways of thinking and behavior when you enter God's kingdom.* Examples: Asked by the Pharisees when the kingdom of God was coming, Jesus answered, "The kingdom of God is not coming with things that can be observed; nor will they say, 'Look, here it is!' or 'There it is!' For, in fact, the kingdom of God is among you" (Luke 17:20–21). Jesus answered Nicodemus, "Very truly, I tell you, no one can see the kingdom of God without being born from above" (John 3:3).

What Helps You to Enter

2. *You enter God's kingdom only by a changed attitude of the heart, not by following a list of religious rules.* Examples: "You hypocrites! Isaiah prophesied rightly about you when he said: 'This people honors me with their lips, but their hearts are far from me; in vain do they worship me, teaching human precepts as doctrines'" (Matthew 15:7–9). In Luke 18:9–14, Jesus contrasts the phony righteousness of the Pharisee who followed all the religious rules with the obvious virtue of the tax collector who had followed no rules but changed his heart.

3. *Concentrating your attention on Christ strengthens your ability to enter and experience God's kingdom in greater fullness.* Examples: "I am the vine, you are the branches" (John 15:5). "Again Jesus spoke to them, saying, 'I am the light of the world. Whoever follows me will never walk in darkness but will have the light of life'" (John 8:12).

4. *Prayer strengthens your ability to enter God's kingdom and experience it more fully.* Examples: "Ask, and it will be given you; search, and you will find; knock, and the door will be opened for you" (Matthew 7:7). In Matthew 6:10, Jesus teaches his disciples to pray for the kingdom to come.

What Restricts You from Entering

5. *You are blocked from entering God's kingdom unless you turn away from self-centeredness.* Examples: "From that time Jesus began to proclaim, 'Repent, for the kingdom of heaven has come near'" (Matthew 4:17). In Matthew 7:13–14, Jesus' metaphor about the narrow gate teaches that those who enter God's kingdom must make a clear choice between two alternatives.

6. *Taking pride in your religious achievements makes it difficult to enter God's kingdom.* Examples: "Whoever becomes humble like this child is the greatest in the kingdom of heaven" (Matthew 18:4). In Matthew 18:1–4, Jesus elaborates on the need for erasing religious pride in order to enter the kingdom.

7. *Financial wealth makes it more difficult for you to enter God's kingdom because your money brings a false sense of power that distracts you from seeking something better.* Examples: "It is easier for a camel to go through the eye of a needle than for someone who is rich to enter the kingdom of God" (Mark 10:25). In Matthew 6:19–34, Jesus urges us to seek first God's kingdom rather than riches, since

putting something else at first priority can block us from our God relationship.

Rewards for Entering

8. *Though self-concern is not your goal, you receive rich rewards by entering God's kingdom.* Examples: "Those who lose their life for my sake, and for the sake of the gospel, will save it" (Mark 8:35). In Matthew 5:1–12, Jesus lists among the Beatitudes numerous rewards for those who enter the kingdom.

9. *Entering God's kingdom gives you a sense of security that comes from believing your personal needs will be taken care of.* Examples: "And even the hairs of your head are all counted. So do not be afraid; you are of more value than many sparrows" (Matthew 10:30–31). In Matthew 6:25–33, Jesus says that we should not be anxious about our need for food and clothing; God will care for us.

10. *Entering God's kingdom releases a new power in your life and thought processes that transcends the normal cause and effect patterns of your environment.* Examples: "Whatever you ask for in prayer with faith, you will receive" (Matthew 21:22). In Luke 9:1–6, Jesus sends the twelve disciples out with the power to heal the sick. In Luke 10:9, he instructs the Seventy to heal the sick and informs them that the kingdom has come to them.

11. *Entering God's kingdom enables you to live joyfully.* Examples: "I have said these things to you so that my joy may be in you, and that your joy may be complete" (John 15:11). In John 10:10, Jesus says, "I came that they may have life, and have it abundantly."

12. *If you enter God's kingdom, you will continue to live in that consciousness beyond the time of physical death.* Examples: "My sheep hear my voice. I know them, and they follow me. I give them eternal life, and they will never perish. No one will snatch them out of my hand" (John

10:27–28). Similar statements appear in Matthew 19:29; 25:46; Mark 10:30; Luke 18:30; John 3:15–16; 4:14; 5:24; 6:27, 40, 47, 54; 10:28; 12:25; and 17:2–3.

By-Products of Entering

13. *Entering God's kingdom gives you increased love and concern for other people.* Examples: "He said to him, 'You shall love the Lord your God with all your heart, and with all your soul, and with all your mind. This is the greatest and first commandment. And a second is like it: You shall love your neighbor as yourself'" (Matthew 22:37–39). In Luke 10:25–37, Jesus used the parable of the good Samaritan to connect loving God with the qualities of neighborliness and mercy, vividly asserting that loving God always involves an increased awareness of and concern for the needs of others.

14. *Entering God's kingdom makes you less judgmental about other people.* Examples: "Do not judge, so that you may not be judged" (Matthew 7:1). In Matthew 13:24–30, Jesus illustrates the principle of leaving judgment to God instead of trying to do it ourselves.

15. *Entering God's kingdom gives you a more forgiving spirit.* Examples: "Then Peter came and said to him, 'Lord, if another member of the church sins against me, how often should I forgive? As many as seven times?' Jesus said to him, 'Not seven times, but, I tell you, seventy-seven times'" (Matthew 18:21–22).

16. *Entering God's kingdom gives you the desire to help other people enter it, too.* Examples: "Go therefore and make disciples of all nations, baptizing them in the name of the Father and of the Son and of the Holy Spirit, and teaching them to obey everything that I have commanded you" (Matthew 28:19–20). In Matthew 18:10–14, he tells a parable about the urgent need to find one lost sheep, even though ninety-nine are safe in the fold.

17. *If you want to enter God's kingdom, you must live a self-giving life.* Examples: "If any want to become my followers, let them deny themselves and take up their cross and follow me" (Matthew 16:24). In Matthew 20:26–28, Jesus says that the person who wants to be greatest among his followers must be the servant of all the other servants.

Requirements for Continuing

18. *If your thinking and actions become self-centered, you can disconnect from God's kingdom.* Examples: "Not everyone who says to me, 'Lord, Lord,' will enter the kingdom of heaven, but only the one who does the will of my Father in heaven" (Matthew 7:21). In Matthew 7:15–27, Jesus illustrates the need for *continued* right attitudes and actions by saying that a tree is known by its fruits, and by telling a story of two different kinds of house builders.

Negative Results of Not Entering

19. *Failing to enter God's kingdom brings you negative results.* Examples: "So it will be at the end of the age. The angels will come out and separate the evil from the righteous and throw them into the furnace of fire, where there will be weeping and gnashing of teeth" (Matthew 13:49–50).

Future Manifestations of God's Kingdom

20. *God's kingdom will at an unspecified future time become more fully and obviously manifested in the whole of creation.* Examples: "Jesus said to him, 'You have said so. But I tell you, from now on you will see the Son of Man seated at the right hand of Power and coming on the clouds of heaven'" (Matthew 26:64). In Matthew 24:3–44, Jesus deals extensively with an end time when the kingdom will become apparent and vividly real to all.